PORTRAIT OF THE DALES

Portrait of
THE DALES

by

NORMAN DUERDEN

Photographs by the Author

ROBERT HALE · LONDON

© *Norman Duerden 1978*

First published in Great Britain 1978

ISBN 0 7091 69116

Robert Hale Limited
Clerkenwell House
Clerkenwell Green
London, EC1

PHOTOSET, PRINTED AND BOUND IN GREAT BRITAIN
BY WEATHERBY WOOLNOUGH, WELLINGBOROUGH, NORTHANTS

CONTENTS

ILLUSTRATIONS

Between pages 32 and 33

Winter in Littondale
Kilnsey Hall
Owlcotes, Littondale
Arncliffe church, Littondale
River Skirfare, near Litton
South arcade, Coverham Abbey
Effigies in Coverham Abbey
Oughtershaw, Wharfedale
Hubberholme church
Penyghent from Winskill
Penyghent Gill
Drystone wall enclosures near Malham Tarn
Iron Age hutment near Penyghent, Ribblesdale
Feizor, near Settle
Celtic wall, Smearsett

Between pages 96 and 97

Cotton grass on millstone grit
Fossil crinoids, Ribblesdale
Mountain avens
Globe flowers, Garsdale
Golden plover, Oxnop Scar
Oystercatcher, Mallerstang
Woodcock
Goldcrest
Kingfisher
Sandpiper, Lune valley
Fox on screes, Feizor
Dalesmen in Widdale
Jack Metcalfe sounds the forest horn, Bainbridge

MAP

I

EVERYMAN'S DALE

THERE IS an irresistible exuberance about the days when spring first rides in on boisterous March wind to the limestone heights above Wharfe River; it is manifest in the woodpecker's reiterated peal of glee, in the daffodils' frantic paroxysm of welcome; it is echoed in the stick-strewn village street where the rooks are busy in Linton's swaying elms – a clamorous exultation of bird and branch and wind.

It was on such a day that I sought the shelter of woodland under a tempestuous sky, a billowing white ceiling driving merrily up-dale towards Kilnsey where a persistent corridor of blue streamed above the crag – a fragment of heaven torn down and held. Beneath the overhang – produced, we are told, as glaciers gouged their way down Wharfedale – jackdaws expostulate and prospect for nest-sites; in the calmer air below the limestone scarp there is much journeying, but occasionally a party of birds in an excess of zeal stray beyond the aerial backwater, and are hurled aloft and scattered, ragged and black, over the grey screes of the hillside.

It is by such natural landmarks that the traveller can mark his progress up or down the valley; they occur as outcrops and eminences, and are found in most of the longer dales. Addleborough and Penhill, in Wensleydale; Kisdon in Swaledale; Ern Crag in Littondale, guarding the approach to Arncliffe; less claustrophobic, Penyghent haunched above Ribblesdale – each has its own character, its own geological niche, dominating the view along miles of dale until with bend in road and river it is hidden by an intervening scrap or spur. Thus the personality of a dale changes as one progresses along it; its different aspects are further increased by changes of light and season. The promontory darkened by cloud shadow and dominant one moment may the next be lost in the general hue; the effect of crops of unusually bright colour is less ephemeral. A field of charlock or buttercups, brilliant under a June sun, may dominate a section of the dale for many days.

In Kilnsey Crag we have a permanent focal point for this section of Wharfedale, and sheltering below the limestone promontory the remains of a village that flourished in monastic times, when much of the property and land were given by Alice de Romilly to Fountains Abbey. What remains of the Hall, now little more than a grey shell, stands behind the Tennant Arms Hotel; close by, one of the best-known drovers' roads, Mastiles Lane, leads off over the scar towards Malham. It was along this lane and its continuation, linking with granges in the Lake District, that livestock were taken; sheep bred in the Dales pastures were driven for long miles along almost continuous drovers' tracks to winter in Borrowdale. The view from the scarp shows to perfection the glacier-levelled floor of the valley, surmounted by limestone heights, mostly pastureland and outcrop. Across the intervening meadowland by the grey roofs of Conistone, and indeed along the visible length of the dale, the grass-grown lynchets of the Anglian arable fields show as terraces along the hillside, best seen under oblique sunlight, or after a light snowfall, when they appear as alternating strips of white and green as a thaw sets in. The terraces, built up in steps along the lower slopes, were made wide enough to be worked by a team of oxen, and for ease of working were mostly horizontal; the lateral arrangement also assisted the conservation of soil on slopes where erosion by rain was considerable.

Today the flat fields below the Crag, cleared by Anglian farmers for their water meadows, are the scene in September of the renowned Kilnsey Show, where you can rub shoulders (as it were) with every aspect of the rural life of the Dales. There are sheep, and horses, and dogs, and those whose life revolves round them. There are cattle parades, racing, and sheepdog trials. Beyond the marquees, refreshments, and livery-stalls a group of bronzed dalesmen in competition are 'setting a wall on its feet'. Sunlight glints on horse brass; a magnificently groomed Swaledale sports a rosette as big as its head; machinery so clean and gaudy in its new paint as to be unreal. It is all larger than life – a living Kodachrome of surpassing brilliance – or rain drives solidly down on to canvas, and grass is churned to a quagmire. Mud-spattered townsfolk from Skipton and Bradford rub shoulders with dalesfolk in crowded marquees. A tannoy charges the atmosphere with a sudden surfeit of sound; there is a momentary lull. "Will Mrs Lister of Gargrave please report . . . ?" "We're short a' nowt wi've got!" announces a robust dalesman with evident satisfaction. Water drips from a battered trilby on to his ham sandwich. Outside the rain is easing off. It would take more than a shower to dampen the ardour of the Kilnsey Show!

Three centuries ago from a vantage point on the Crag the glance would have passed over almost continuous woodland in the direction of Threshfield; now all that remains is a small section at that glorious bend of the river above Grassington where the long reach of the dale, revealed above a margin of white shingle, carries the perpetual promise of a good day ahead. Most of Kilnsey Wood and all of its deer are long gone, but this little corner is not without interest. In winter and early spring, nuthatches on their daily patrols through Grass Wood, where they are fed by visitors, cross the river and forage in the great beech trees. May brings its tree pipits to the overgrown bank, and the evocative trill of the wood warbler is sometimes heard from high among newly opened sprays of the beeches. One May morning at the edge of the wood, I unexpectedly flushed a sandpiper from her nest beside a bracken frond. As the bird made off with arched wings, half running, half flying, she passed by the bright orange wall of a canvas pavilion, which along with a car and trailer, and assorted domestic impedimenta, had planted itself overnight a few yards from the water's edge. It is a great pity, especially in a National Park, that such a splendid viewpoint should be spoilt by indiscriminate migration of this sort; personally, on a spring morning outdoors I can do very well without the transistorized deliberations of James Young Esq. (good fellow though he may be!) and the unsanitary sorties of an over-nourished corgi. Across the river in the Grass Wood reserve bird and flower flourish in sacrosanct immunity, but the sandpipers and oystercatchers of the shingle bank at its edge must take 'pot luck' with the common herd. This they often do with some success, which is surprising in a dale that has

more visitors than most. One of the most bewildering anomalies in our National Parks is that of 'conservation' and
private interest. In one protected area along the Wharfe,
visitors to the nature trails are exhorted not to interfere with
wild life or to pick flowers. When I arrived there one winter
morning, woodsmen were busy with tractors removing a
whole section of mature woodland; the woods are, of course,
privately owned. In another dale, forests of conifers are being
established on fellsides, and limestone pavement is torn out by
bulldozers and sold. It is all very confusing, and not a little
disheartening. In so many cases there seems to be little one
can do; rocks, hedges and trees are not easily replaced. Nor is
the threat always brought about wilfully; unwitting inter-
ference and changes in habitat inevitably take their toll.

Perhaps some rethinking will have to be done by both sides
– conservationists and general public. In a limestone area
which shall be nameless a dedicated watcher sits on guard for
a period of the year over a small colony of orchids that seems
to have become the perquisite of the erudite and the organized; which says much for the enthusiasm of the watcher, but
perhaps less for the idea that prompts the vigil. One can, I
fancy, detect a certain parallel between Lakeland's struggling
eagles and the lady's slipper orchid of the Dales upland. Much
sentiment, but little expectation. I hope I am proved wrong.

At Grass and Bastow Woods too, some felling has recently
taken place, but without undue effect on the varied flora of
the reserve, which includes lily of the valley, fly orchis,
Solomon's seal, and herb paris. Of birds, jay, bullfinch, willow
tit, marsh tit, nuthatch and great spotted woodpecker may be
looked for, and at dusk in springtime the prolonged 'roding'
excursions of the woodcock. His uncertain flight, with bill
inclined downwards, occurs regularly hereabouts, following
the curve of the river, where the bird's squeak and croaking
may be heard above the tree-tops, continuing to the very
edge of night. It is a unique experience to climb the wooded
scarp on an April evening and listen to the birds passing at
eye-level before one.

To the regular visitor it is probably not the official sanctuaries that in the long run afford most pleasure, but the
interesting corners of the dales discovered almost accidentally
over the years; village, copse, or roadside verge, which in their

season give especial pleasure. There is one spot, for example, on the heights above Kettlewell, where in June the brilliant blood-red cranesbill blooms; a place of pilgrimage in a deep ravine in Littondale where mountain avens are to be seen in their southernmost station in England; and a delightful reach of the Skirfare where oystercatcher and sandpiper nest among a profusion of flowers. Or it may be the pleasure of a view-point, like the one at Hesleden High Bergh, with the length of Littondale at one's feet. Of villages, Arncliffe, Hawkswick and Conistone come to mind, though many hamlets are losing their character. Linton is a gem, whose inhabitants give one the impression of being possessed of a wanderlust; in few villages can they demonstrate more ways of getting across a river than here, where, in a short length of stream, road, clapper, and pack-horse bridges are separated by a ford! Perhaps there is some magical significance in crossing the water!

The praises of Thorpe, the 'secret hidden village', with its dubious legends of shoemakers and the occult, have been sung by writers from Halliwell Sutcliffe onwards. I first came to it on a raw and misty February day along the narrow lane that leads by Threapland below the reef-knolls of Skelterton, and Stebden - modest, rounded hills, shrouded on this day with a shapeless grey blanket of cloud. Moss-encrusted walls of lime-stone, imprinted here and there with the fossil remains of crinoids, lead one down to Thorpe. It was one of those days when winter seems determined to erase all signs of spring. But the signs were there, in the first early halting song of the chaffinch - "Will you, will you . . . kiss me . . . (dear)?" - the last word as yet very uncertain!; in the newly born lambs, also very uncertain of themselves; and in the white encap-sulated snowdrop buds, appearing almost apologetically on the bank. Where the lane was at its narrowest there came another 'rustle of spring' - the song of a tractor. A farmer's wife appeared, on foot: "Look out! He's coming with a muck-spreader," she cautioned. I scrambled on to the wall; evidently pedestrians were not to be reckoned with in these parts. Far be it from me to delay the coming of spring, whatever form its advent may take!

The village lies in a hollow, sheltered by the knolls of Elbolton and Kail. In summer, canopied by foliage, the setting must be idyllic, but in the chill and damp of this February day, Thorpe 'sub montem' seemed strangely quiet and scarcely impressive – a sort of Wycoller, with people.

> Sweet smiling village, loveliest of the lawn,
> Thy sports are fled, and all thy charms withdrawn.

Probably its charms are reserved for that part of the year that lies between the daffodils and Michaelmas daisies.

Two miles away from the seclusion of Thorpe, all roads converge on Grassington, bustling tourist centre of the upper dale. Formerly a market, it was concerned during the last century with lead mining and textiles; with the coming of the Yorkshire Dales Railway in 1901, it became a dormitory town for workers in Bradford. Today, visitors from Pittsburg and Potter's Bar wine and dine, and make the tour of fashionable shops in the square.

On a summer day the narrow street that leads to Yarnbury is chock-a-block with holiday-makers. Limousines and Land-rovers manoeuvre miraculously between stone cottages; a few more shops, a coffee house, and the road to the hills is before you. A phalanx of school-children from Nelson, each slung with haversack and project-board, crocodile their way behind an incredibly youthful teacher, off to see the remains of an Iron Age village on the hillside. Beyond Yarnbury, the scarred face of Grassington Moor stretches away in an impressive chaos of spoil heap, smelt mill, and derelict working. Here there are none for company but wheatear and industrial archaeologist; from the shelter of the gullies where Blea Beck and Groove Gill cut down off Hebden Moor, the reiterated whistle of the ring ouzel becomes a part of the silence. In an area blessed with such a wealth of outward beauty as Craven, the forces of darkness are in no way precluded from its traditions, and are commemorated in legend and place names; as, for example, at Boggart's Hole, Yorda's Cave and Trow Gill. The erosion of the permeable limestone into caves and potholes lends itself to stories, possibly of Scandinavian origin, of ghosts and barguests who were held to frequent such grottoes. Near Hebden is the notorious Dibbles (Devil's) Bridge, where, as legend has it, Martin Calvert fought and beat the Devil; and a mile or so from the village of Appletreewick, the spectacular limestone ravine of Troller's Gill looks up at Barden Fell.

As Kilnsey Crag marks a stage of progression along the upper dale, so these lower reaches of Wharfe River are dominated by the outcrop on Barden Fell of Simon's Seat, a fine viewpoint of exposed rocks from which the changing character of Wharfedale is eloquently displayed. Indeed, the view from the fell epitomizes the charm of the Yorkshire Dales as a whole, an appeal which lies in the constant interplay of limestone and gritstone. The underlying geological sequences are reflected in the upland profiles, the flora and fauna, and in the pattern of farming, buildings, and industry of the area. From Simon's Seat we can look south and west upon a section of the dale patently of millstone grit; dark and weathered outcrops above Embsay; bracken and heather slopes, and the call of grouse; peat moor, bilberry edge, cotton grass, and foxglove. To the north and north-west, one notices the gradual enclosing of the dale within limestone scarps, and the delicate 'stepped' terraces of the Yoredale Series of limestone, shale and sandstone. Upper Wharfedale is predominantly limestone country, if one excludes the highest ground, as, for example, the Whernsides and Buckden Pike. A closer examination would reveal a change of vegetation, with an abundance of ash trees, often in lines along the terraces, and a prolific flora which includes cranesbills, rock roses, milkwort, mountain pansy, and a number of orchids. An approach to the Dales by way of the Wharfe and Simon's Seat is certainly a fine introduction to the land form and natural history of these Pennines.

Below this viewpoint, and the neighbouring Earl's Seat, is the ruinous grey tower of Barden. Built by Lord Henry Clifford, and repaired some two hundred years later by Lady Anne Clifford in 1657, it has since suffered mixed fortunes; today the structure, once the site of a hunting lodge, is one of Wharfedale's picturesque ruins. Equally attractive to artist and photographer, Barden Bridge close by carries the visitor by back roads to Howgill, Harthington and Burnsall, or by App'trick to Pately Bridge and Nidderdale.

Below the bridge in Bolton Woods, Wharfe River passes in tumult through a narrow gorge of rocks. 'The Strid' has claimed many victims, not the least illustrious being the son

of landowner Alice de Romilly – the Boy of Egremond –
who came to grief while attempting to cross the ravine; the
legend is retold by Wordsworth in 'The Force of Prayer'.
However apocryphal the story may be, the name of young
Romilly does appear on title deeds when, through a gift of
land by his mother, Augustinian canons came to Bolton in
1155, relinquishing the austerity of a previous site on Embsay
Moor.

It is small wonder that Bolton Abbey (or Bolton Priory, to
be more correct), set by wooded slopes in a great curve of the
river, should have inspired poet and writer: Turner, Cox,
Girtin, Landseer and Ruskin were among those who were
impressed by the idyllic beauty of the Priory, of which only
the nave of the church is still in use. Architectural features
range from the dogtooth ornament of the Early English style
to Decorated tracery in the transept windows. Two thirteenth-
century doorways give access to a sunken cloister, marked by
a low, moss-covered wall; in May wallflowers and toadflax
decorate the stones of the transept; and the chapter house has
been usurped by an ash tree. In the outer wall a nuthatch
rears her young in a crevice in the masonry. So has nature
embellished a setting already revered; a setting completely in
accord with the ethos of the same Victorian romanticism that
urged the use of convex 'landscape mirrors', and required
viewpoints along the Wharfe to be named, as at 'Clifford
Seat', and 'Strid Seat'. On a wave of enthusiasm brought
about by improved communications and the growing interest
of working people in the outdoors, wagonettes plied from
Skipton Station along the road to Wharfedale; horses and
carriages could be hired at main centres for conveying visitors
"to all Places of Interest in the Neighbourhood". It is perhaps
significant to note that in 1890 one could travel by horse bus
from Skipton to Grassington for one shilling – a quarter of
the price currently charged for leaving one's car in the car
park at Bolton Abbey!

The practice of tourism, then, is nothing new, but the lapse
of a century has replaced the landscape mirror with a Kodak
'Instamatic', and visitors now arrive in more comfortable
conveyances, mass-produced perhaps on the other side of the
world!

Although the Priory suffered more from mismanagement,

the Scots and King Henry's Commissioners, than ever it has
done since at the hands of tourists, at the height of the season
one sometimes gets the feeling that, like Aysgarth, Malham
Cove and Fountains Abbey, Bolton has perhaps been over-
exposed to tourism.

Those who love quiet may prefer to come in springtime,
taking refuge in the fastnesses of woods which will presently
echo to the sound of the human voice, as summer visitors
explore the many nature trails. But for the present there is
peace for the lone country lover intent on pleasantly losing
himself among April's increasing greenery. Sitting in an
elevated corner of woodland at Strid he hears the sound of
Wharfe River below – a constant murmurous undertone of
water released from hollow depths of rock, too distant to be
intrusive. In the April sunshine it seems that the entire avian
orchestra is now attuned to the tempo of spring. From the
edge of the wood comes the crowing of a cock pheasant
presently glimpsed between smooth peeling bars of birch fencing; rings of bark litter the ground, silver sleeves displaced
from the horizontal boles. Besides being a beautiful tree, birch
is a useful one on the estate, and one particularly attractive,
especially in decay, to birds. Branchless boles are sometimes
riddled with nesting holes of the great spotted woodpecker,
one beneath the other, each representing a past breeding
season. The bird begins at the top, working downwards and
round, though some borings are merely exploratory; bracket
fungus protrudes, the upper older growths hard and discoloured. Now the woodpecker adds his own touch of percussion,
drumming sporadically from the sounding-board of a nearby
branch. His activities day by day are brought to a focus on
one particular tree beneath which a sprinkling of wood-chips
is becoming noticeable.

Jay and crow, too, are increasingly vocal, producing some
surprising un-crow-like variations of note. From the depths
of the wood a carrion crow blows his 'motor horn'; the harsh
answer sounds alarmingly close from the tree-tops almost
above my head. Few things escape the eye of this bird, but
like the pigeon which sometimes pitches immediately over-
head, he finds it difficult to look directly downwards. The
harsh calling continues, and is presently punctuated by the
more distinct bleating of a lamb. For a time the duet con-

tinues, bass and coloratura. There is a touch of dark comedy about these few moments of April. A few feet from me a dead oak leaf has been pierced and lifted by the spear of a bluebell; it flutters like a pennant, several inches from the ground, and in so doing marks the bittersweet moment of a spring at its zenith.

II

THE FLOWERY DALE

BEYOND GRASSINGTON and the limits of the main dale there is a growing feeling of isolation. The narrowing confines of the valley floor and the Wharfe's lesser tributaries, cutting back into limestone gills to peter out among the peat hags and solitudes of Great Whernside and Buckden Pike, add to the impression of wildness. Indeed, in any side dale which does not carry a good 'through' road there is this feeling of remoteness. Littondale, though technically not a 'blind' dale, certainly comes into this category in spite of two gated upland roads that permit escape to Malham and Ribblesdale. They climb across the shoulders of Fountains Fell and Penyghent; from the eastern slopes of Darnbrook Fell, or, better still, from the Berghs ('Barks') above Halton Gill, the enclosed nature of the glacier-gouged valley becomes even more apparent. Watered by the River Skirfare, which joins the Wharfe at Ammerdale Dub, the relatively straight dale runs for nine miles to the hamlet of Foxup, which like Halton Gill, Litton and Arncliffe was once a hunting-lodge in the Foreſt of Litton. During the twelfth and thirteenth centuries when much of the uplands of Craven passed into the hands of the monasteries, Littondale was granted to Fountains and Salley, and enlarged lodges became the present-day hamlets and villages, with granges also at Hawkswick, Owlcotes, Hesleden, and Cosh. In spite of a high degree of organization in the running of the dale, affairs did not always go smoothly; poaching and trespass were rife, and there was rivalry between the two religious houses, as, for example, over the use of the mill at Litton where land was contiguous.

The many reminders of monastic days found on every hand – drovers' roads, grange, and ruined abbey – are not the only remains that will appeal to the student; these Pennine hills afford opportunity to observe a variety of sites at first hand. In the outcrops, fossiliferous rocks, and caves of Craven one can get an insight into geological times; some caverns like Elbolton,

19

in Wharfedale, and Victoria Cave above Settle, have in their remains given us a glimpse of prehistory. From the hillside by Douky Bottom Cave one can look across Littondale towards what must surely be one of the most historically comprehensive views in the Dales. There, below the scarp of Old Cote Moor, nestles the village of Hawkswick, with its Norse and medieval connotations; east of it on the boulder-strewn hillside below the scarp one can perceive a number of small rectangular enclosures, picked out, as it were, in a sort of grassy Braille. The remains of this Iron Age Village are best seen in low morning sunlight, or after a light snowfall. Below are the grassed-over terraces of an Anglian townfield, themselves intersected with enclosures of drystone walling. A modern road with cattle grids and traffic signs gives access to the village. In Hawkswick itself there is scarcely room by the river for houses; barn doors open towards the water's edge and one can sit and watch ducks from the breakfast table. Limestone scarp and outcrop, and scrub woodland, carpeted in spring with primroses, rear up beyond the hamlet.

If flowers are your delight you will find your spiritual home here in Littondale, arguably the finest dale, botanically, in England; but "Medea's wonderful alchemy" is not always as prompt or as evenly distributed as one might expect. It is well to remember that here, as in most easterly areas, spring can be a laggard.

On the western side of the dale, rising like a wall above the green corridor of valley floor, high scarps exclude the sun for long periods of the year; under these cooler conditions, as, for example, at Scoska, it is possible to come across stitchwort and dog violets blooming in June. One of the most beautiful sights I ever saw was the emergence of a family of freshly-dry sandpiper chicks from a scrape set in the midst of a bank of primroses in full bloom. Perhaps it was all part of the magic of Midsummer Day!

There are many magical moments for the flower-lover in Littondale, where a lengthy list of 'calcicoles' – lime-loving plants – includes rock rose, milkwort, bird's-eye primrose, hart's-tongue fern, spleenwort and common polypody. The cranesbills are well represented, and include the less common blood-red form, and the dale is not without its rarities; on the steep slopes of a nearby gill the mountain aven, which Professor

Pearsall describes as "one of the most striking of mountain plants," is to be seen in its southernmost station in England.

Naturalists, fishermen, and sightseers come in summer to Arncliffe, principal village of Littondale, and in so many ways the archetype of all Dales villages; thanks to enthusiastic writers and television, it is now better known, perhaps, than at any time in its history. One can enjoy the hospitality of The Falcon, a delightfully unpretentious country inn, or admire the village green with its row of grey stone houses whose outline fits so beautifully beneath the enclosing scarp. One is tempted to imagine what the place was like before the petrol engine revolutionized the rural way of life – a hundred and fifty years ago, perhaps, when the hamlet was visited by Tom Airey and his group of theatrical players; or even earlier, when, unlikely as it might seem today, a cotton mill flourished here. For those villagers without a car, there can still be problems. One day I chatted with an old man working on the green. Asked about the isolation of the village, he informed me: "We allus git stocked up for winter – a bagga two taties, bacon and that! Ther's only one bus a week, ta Skipton, and if ya miss that, ya've ta 'ave another week's 'oliday!" However, he reassured me that while the grocery cart came only once a month from Skipton, the beer arrived "twice a week" – obviously an essential commodity!

Above the noisy River Skirfare at Arncliffe the artist is as close to perfection as he is ever likely to be. By the bridge a church set among snowdrops and aconites is so taken by its own beauty that it retires from view at daffodil-time, unheeded behind a green and thickening canopy where the blackbird whistles away summer. Indeed, it is the setting and historical background of St Oswald's that are its main attractions, for only the tower remains of the fifteenth-century building, and the visitor will find little of architectural interest in the Victorian reconstruction of nave and chancel on Norman foundations.

There are sometimes days of brilliance that come in February which carry with them all the promise of a new and unusual season. Snowy scarp top, dazzling under an unclouded sky of deepest blue, gives to the landscape that touch of drama that always accompanies a reversal of tone values, as of blackthorn blossom seen against the leaden shower cloud of April.

Snowdrops, drifted thickly against graveless headstones, are equally compelling to the eye here in the churchyard. A net of shadows is cast on the white face of the church tower, a rectangle of light trapped in the mesh of sycamores. Exuberant chaffinch and watchful nuthatch, ever on duty above the lych-gate, announce the time of year as unmistakenly as the clock in the tower tells the time of day.

Inside the building, gloomy now as in Norman times, one realizes that the church in Arncliffe is considerably older than the fabric. The first recorded rector held office about 1180, when the dale was a hunting forest. Eagles (or 'Ernes') nested close by, if the implication of the name 'Arncliffe' is correct; and squirrels from Cosh, at the dale head, could, it is said, visit their relatives at Strid without once touching the ground! On the nave wall a decorated muster-list records the names of local lads who bore arms at Flodden Field in 1513: 'Knolle, - able, horsed and harnished"; "Frnklyn - a bowe"; "Tennant - a bille"; and so on. A Book of Remembrance open at the month of February catches the eye, as does the name displayed - that of Marmaduke Miller, who died in February 1970. Many are the folk who recall with affection the renowned 'M'duke - angler, painter, and sometime proprietor of The Falcon Inn.

Now the artist on the bridge, thankfully doffing his mittens, paints in comfort, making the most of light and atmosphere; this little spot by the river is a place of pilgrimage. Here painter and photographer alike work on quietly and patiently, exercising the ability to look closely and critically, which is the key to the fullest appreciation of the outdoors. They note the play of light on the scarp beyond the church tower; the purposeful flight of the dipper, backwards and forwards under the bridge; the telling lines of cast-shadow that dance across the sunlit face of the tower. If the church is dedicated to St Oswald, the bridge must surely come under the protection of Messrs Rowney and Kodak!

Upstream, the view is no less attractive. A delightful house, Bridge End, presides over its snowdrops and wagtails on the river bank, "in a fairy tale come true". Those of a literary turn of mind will no doubt speculate on its associations with Charles Kingsley and *The Water Babies*, for it was to this house that the writer, a guest of Walter Morrison at Malham Tarn House, came as a visitor.

A quiet, silent, rich happy place is Vendale . . . three hundred
feet of limestone terraces, one below the other, as straight as if they
had been ruled with a ruler and then cut out with a chisel . . .
First, a little grass-slope, covered with the prettiest flowers;
rock-rose and saxifrage, and thyme and basil, and all sorts of sweet
herbs. Then bump down a two foot step of limestone.
Then another bit of grass and flowers.

No great stretch of the imagination is required to set *The Water
Babies* in a context of Bridge End and Littondale.

In hill country, the finest prospects are usually to be had
from viewpoints a few hundred feet above the valley; from the
many limestone terraces at about a thousand feet the widening
panorama reveals new features at every step; blue tarns, unfamiliar outcrops, a glimpse of grass tracks that trace their
undulating parallels across the upland. Their purpose and
direction are often not apparent today, except where a section
of modern road has been superimposed in the present century.
There are monastic roads, and drovers' and packhorse tracks;
the 'market road' that linked Ribblesdale and Wensleydale
passed from Arncliffe by Cowside Beck, Malham Moor and
Langcliffe to Settle, a market town since Norman times. Early
in the eighteenth century the town was granted additional fairs
and the market augmented; livestock and produce were
brought across the hills by track and bridle-path from remoter
dales. Cloth, leather and vegetables were offered for sale; "oate
meal", scarcer in the west, was in much demand. Apparently
not all needs were utilitarian. The botanist Curtis records the
purchase, in 1781, of ten lady's slipper orchids from a man who
offered a bunch of about forty at Settle's flourishing market.

On the east of Cowside Beck a track known as Monks'
Road passes from Arncliffe to Malham by way of the Clowder
(Old English 'clud', a mass of rock or hill) and Middle House.
A narrow lane – a place of mimulus in high summer – winds
away from The Falcon to peter out beneath the scarp. A
pleasant spot, even in early March, when the golden days of
mimulus are just a dream. A blackbird preceding me along the
muddy track perches momentarily on a post, feathers ruffled, a
black apron blown about its shoulders – then clatters away
behind the wall. Scilla and crocus have appeared, overnight it
seems, in the cottage garden, beguiled by the hazy sunshine.

As I pass the croft a workman in council livery, a vision of orange fluorescence, appears, bearing a bin; somehow the idyll of Arncliffe does not include a refuse-cart.

"Ya can't git ower Darnbrook - bridge is down. Ya'll 'a' ta walk!" he volunteers.

I assure him I have no intention of crossing Cowside Beck, and press on for Monks' Road. A tractor, busy as a bee, drones from village to pasture, and back again. The aroma that rises to the scarp has a hint of pineapple, and is in its way as evocative of the end of winter as the fragrance of bluebells that herald the coming of summer.

At eleven hundred feet the slope levels off on to a delectable plateau of grassland that might have been designed for walking. The light wind, still sharpened with a touch of the east, is merely pleasant after the effort of climbing. Along the edge of the hill a number of rills, ever victims of the wayward permeable limestone, appear and disappear in a matter of yards; their course is marked by a darker fringe of grasses and by the subdued undertones of running water - an unusual sound on limestone uplands. East wind across the heights has a way of modifying sound - a connection at first not, perhaps, apparent. The same vapour that drains the blue from the sky and softens distances in windy weather has a similar effect upon the hearing. A veil of atmosphere hangs about the deep ravine of Cowside, concealing yet revealing; from the uncertain outlines of Darnbrook Fell the imagination can move unchecked into the further recesses of the dale. Under these conditions, on the rock terraces there is a sense of timelessness that turns back the centuries, and one pictures the shivering Celt peering on such a morning as this from the doorway of his hut, and cursing his arthritis. One wonders if he, too, noted with relief the re-appearance on the heights of lark and lapwing or rejoiced at the piping of golden plovers newly returned to the slopes above his sheep pens. Now in the silver haze the plovers gather in the fields of Darnbrook, and the contralto trilling of birds already dispersed to breeding grounds is heard in the grey lands above Cowside. In these early days at the turn of the season, and under less luminous skies, the gorgeous gold-speckled birds appear duller and browner and are easily overlooked, especially when feeding in small flocks. They are usually revealed, however, by the plaintive whistle, particularly insistent when the birds have reached their breeding pitches and are more demonstrative.

At one point along Monks' Road to Middle House the path dips steeply to negotiate a gully that drains into Cowside Beck, some hundreds of feet below. Presently the track, winding by wall and outcrop, emerges on to Dewbottoms, where on a natural rampart of limestone terracing the stone-banked enclosures and tumbledown huts of an early homestead mark the activities of some Celtic family of farmers who eked out their existence in a miserably hostile climate. The settlement dates from the late Bronze or early Iron Age, and includes at least one large field and several smaller ones. Many of the stone ramparts around the sunken enclosures are still in fair condition. One can step over what once might have been a stockade and can clearly trace among the natural outcrops the outline of fields. A concentration of stones here and there marks the position of a hut; these are mostly circular, and are sometimes set in the angle of two walls. In one the entrance, perhaps originally covered with a skin, is plainly visible. As I approach, a startled sheep leaves by it, and runs off down the hillside. Another hut contains a number of dead thistles, and the skeleton of a rabbit. It is almost two thousand years since early man penned his sheep, goats, cattle, and perhaps horses, in these enclosures, or tended his little plot of oats on the dry terraces above Littondale. There is something more impressive about a winter day at Dewbottoms than all the spectacle of Gordale Scar or the falls of Ingleton, which lack the compulsive appeal of human associations.

Monks' Road is not always the easiest of tracks to follow, and has many ramifications. Not to be recommended is that which for a difficult and precarious mile skirts the base of the limestone edge and totters its uncertain way above Yew Cogar Scar. If ever monk trod this path he must have done so with girded loins, at risk of life and limb; it is certainly no exercise for the inactive, or for those of nervous disposition. Nor, for that matter, is it a route for sandalled feet! There are times when the path disappears completely; but here and there a chipped stone shows that one is not the first to tread these exposed screes. As Arncliffe comes into view over the shoulder of the scarp, the incline becomes less severe, and the walker can survey the scene with equanimity, noting the windings of

Cowside Beck, stone walls at an incredible angle, and a likely shingle bank below beloved of oystercatchers. It is a relief to the ankles to set foot once again on the level lane that leads to the village, and one is tempted to give credence to the story that dalesmen are born with legs of unequal length as a concession against the exigencies of their environment!

There are some corners of the Dales to which the over-worked adjective 'idyllic' can justifiably be applied, and in this respect Littondale qualifies with distinction, especially in its upper reaches:

> the haunt
> Of every gentle wind, whose breath can teach
> The wilds to love tranquillity.

For a mile or more above Litton the Skirfare, in deference to the rural quiet, goes underground; ash and sycamore are mirrored in static pools left in the hollows of its bleached slabs, and the dipper is an outcast. Dales rivers usually conform to the character of the dale through which they flow, and Skirfare is no exception, yet the dale has a thousand lesser voices. Some emanate from impressive limestone gills; others make their entrance quietly, almost apologetically, and are absorbed un-noticed. Such becks are, as far as map-makers are concerned, undistinguished and nameless, yet to the countrygoer are often most rewarding.

Down the hillside they show as a thin trickle of water scarcely noticeable from the valley floor; after rain their course is more marked. White plumes show where the beck passes over a rocky outcrop in a series of miniature cascades, but the spectacle is temporary. On these limestone scarps much of the effect is soon lost due to the permeability of the rock, and streams are prone to disappear altogether. Sometimes those that survive reach the flood plains of the main river with a final burst of enthusiasm, as here in Littondale, cascading through some tiny gorge or screened by scrub woodland which softens the sound of their exuberance. The waterfall known simply as 'Foss' issues from a cave below Scoska Moor in Old Litton, which lies across the river from the present-day hamlet. At other times tributaries steal surreptitiously across the valley floor beneath bridges and tree roots, or end their days in some ignominious culvert.

The hamlet of Litton, with its ancient cottages, The Queen's Arms, and a strip of green, lies between two not inconsiderable gills, Potts Beck and Crystal Beck; a maze of lanes and paths lead down to the river. In summer white umbels of sweet cicely spread shoulder high along walled tracks, and the unmistakable fragrance of aniseed lingers on the clothing. One can explore up-dale along a highway of dry river bed, or can cross to Spittle Croft, once perhaps a monastic hospice, on the old track to Stainforth and Settle. By the bridge, a rare place for sandpipers – a marker indicates flood level at a remarkable height when one considers the normally dry river bed; but beneath the bridge the force of water in times of spate is hinted at by a cavernous pothole excavated in the limestone bed.

Of all the prospects of Littondale's ultimate oases that of Halton Gill from the 'berghs' is undoubtedly the one to play upon the heartstrings; to come upon it suddenly, in the first flush of June, and descend to it at a contemplative saunter by outcrop and buttercup field, is to experience all that is best in the Pennine idiom. But no sybarite ever earned the full freedom of the dale, and you must come to it at all seasons, in all weathers, under all sorts of skies. The most uncompromising of days is seldom without some compensation, with the dale-head scarcely less evocative than in the halcyon days of summer.

Take, for example, the mad March day when in defiance of a weather chart that had all the subtlety of a draughtboard I forsook the indifferent skies of Ribblesdale for the leaden austerity of a dark Penyghent, and an even severer Fountains Fell; between the two a wisp of pale blue hung over Littondale and the hail-encrusted road that leads to Hesleden. On the bergh a trailing curtain of vapour was drawn aside to reveal a cluster of roof-tops, dark above the perceptibly lightening outcrop of limestone.

At Halton Gill you can count the number of houses on the fingers of your hands. Most of them date from the seventeenth century. The datestones '1626 M.K.' and 'C.D. – I.A. 1641' over Low House and the Hall commemorate the Knowles and the Dawsons respectively. One wonders if the Lady Anne Clifford approved of all this new property in the dales; grit-stone blocks, clean and new, like the rash of present-day 'conversions' wrought by off-comers in many of the more accessible villages. Neatly enclosed by the roadside an extension to the chapel-of-ease bears the date 1626 and recalls Henry Fawcett, an exiled son of the dale who in 1619 left an annuity of £10 to the clergyman of Halton Gill for "reading the services and for teaching poor men's children". Brother William supplemented this by a further gift in 1630, a tiny schoolroom being added, whose roof contained a "great measure of oak". It appears that girls came off rather badly at the school. In 1791, following an enquiry from Thomas Lindley, curate of Halton Gill, the vicar of Arncliffe decreed that "the Female children of a Parish cannot be the objects of a Grammar School". As a concession, and for a small fee, they were permitted the simpler blessings of writing and arithmetic. Behind the chapel a track marked 'Hawes' zigzags up the hillside and climbs to almost 2,000 feet on Horse Head Pass and the way to Langstrothdale. It was along this track that Lindley passed each Sunday after service at Halton Gill to serve the chapel at Hubberholme, in the days when men could use their legs. Today the pass is used by ramblers; the pleasant gill above the hamlet, set in its walls and screes of limestone, is deserted. A miniature cascade leaps down in the deep shadow of sycamores, and the sitting ring ouzel can look down from her crevice at a timeless cameo of village life. On reflection, one realizes that there have, of course, been changes. A barn with an arched porch dates from (only) 1829. Since that time the population has declined from 88 to 37 at the 1961 census. In 1958 the school was closed, and its handful of children now study the metric system among snowdrops at Arncliffe. A large modern barn stands next to its elegant Victorian counterpart, and the red dot seen in winter from a distant hillside turns out to be a telephone kiosk. On the land the red tractor, the blue poly-thene bag, and a coil of fencing wire would seem to make all things possible. Even weather comes by courtesy of Yorkshire Television. But such changes are not peculiar to Halton Gill, and in no way detract from "the charm of this enchanted ground".

The whole area of the dale head is dominated by the mass of Penyghent, whose flanks stretch north and east towards Langstrothdale; the head of Littondale is thus enclosed with ridges of millstone grit surmounting terraces of limestone. It is in the heart of this hill country at 1,200 feet that the long road up-dale comes to an end at the hamlet of Foxup – the 'valley of the fox', where the Skirfare is born from the waters of Foxup and Cosh Becks. Here one converses against a perpetual back-ground of running water. At one point, you can see all of three houses, but the dearth of human habitation is more than made up for by an excess of stone walls. The hamlet would have been better named after a bird than a fox, for never was there such a wagtail's delight! Walls enclose the beck; stone bridges lead into farmyards; stone barns rise above a maze of drystone walls. It is the stoniest place you ever saw! Add to these the frantic barking of two dogs (each the guardian of a bridge), the tumult of a swollen beck, the sound of a tractor and tank, and the rattle of hail on a tin roof, and you will gather that Foxup is not the dreamiest of places on a boisterous March morning. The very signposts appear to have called up their reinforce-ments in a visual frenzy of helpful directions – 'Horton-in-Ribblesdale'; 'Nether Hesleden' and 'Litton'; a track beyond the hamlet leads to Birkwith.

Nor are the birds less demonstrative as I take to the fellside beyond the sign 'To Cosh'. An exuberant missel thrush, the "trumpeter of March", hurls out his welcome to spring; passing hailstorm and distant sliver of snow on Far Bergh are alike beneath his notice. Migrating fieldfares – a huge flock – trail away in small parties, for a mile along the beck, as if reluctant to be disturbed; but with the first shuttlecock song-flight of the meadow pipit their days are numbered. The rain squall passes, and a pale fitful shadow dances ahead of me on the glistening slabs of limestone.

"Chucka, chuck," from the ash-tops.

"Peeowitt-pu," from a lapwing.

"Too-li a li a li," from the soaking pasture.

Redshank is back too.

And then, the first glorious bubbling cadence of a curlew – it is almost nine months since those exquisite notes were heard above the sound of the beck at Foxup. There are stirring days in March along the track that leads to the "loneliest house in England".

At a second gate a pattern of walling becomes discernible on the far hillside, and the unexpected green of intake relieves the rough slopes; a third gate, and above my shadow, now clear-cut, a chimney pot rises as if from the ground itself.

Cosh, set in a lonely hollow, is as remote as its Scandinavian name implies – 'kosh', a shepherd's mountain hut. At almost fifteen hundred feet a moss-covered sycamore, and, unbelievably, an elm, flank the shell of a house or barn amid a confusion of drystone walls. By an overgrown croft a beck still tumbles as a little waterfall across the hamlet's centre. It is over twenty years since the main house was occupied, and a century or more since the three houses at Cosh flourished as a self-supporting community where weaving and spinning were carried on. Today, surprisingly, there are signs that some life is returning, though perhaps not permanently. The cottage sports a bright blue door, and beneath a green lintel a nameplate that would send the Postmaster General into transports of delight announces: "Cosh – No. 1". Regrettably, there is no indication of a postal code!

As I sit behind a wall wind-dodging, a flurry of rain reminds me that I have the best part of an hour's walk still before me. At gate one the heavens open. At gate two, I am wet. By gate three, I have ceased to care. At the final gate, I stop to exchange a word with a farmer who has emerged from the cloud and overtaken me in a Landrover. I express surprise that anyone should be out on the hills in such weather.

"Ah've nine hundred Swaled'ls out on't fell, and they're lambin' in a fortnit," he replies dryly.

Perhaps surprisingly, the fell is farmed from Birkwith, in Ribblesdale – a journey of nearly twenty miles around Penyghent. At gathering-time shepherds work in pairs, with dogs, and drive the sheep across the fells direct to the home farm.

Cosh may well be the loneliest spot in England, but not if you happen to be a sheep!

III

PAGES OF HISTORY

Beautiful Wharfedale, so sweet and so fair,
Nowhere in England can with thee compare.

WHARFEDALE is beautiful; let no one deny it. Scarcely less so, one imagines, than in the early days of the century, when William Foster of Beckermonds wrote the above lines. To take the track by Kilnsey in all the splendour of summer, with ash trees burgeoning and meadows carpeted with flowers, is to see limestone landscape at its best. June brings the summer – the rock roses; the swallows; and the visitors, in a constant and sometimes overwhelming flow, from the industrial towns that lie to the south. And who can blame them? Turner, Gray, Girtin and Wordsworth knew the dale, and revealed its beauty; and beauty has almost been its undoing. Unless you know the place intimately – its upland tracks and corners of woodland – you may find yourself wishing for the quieter hours of winter.

Grassington and Kettlewell have borne the brunt of these annual invasions since the days when Thomas Septimus Airey ran his conveyances between the two villages each day, and wagonettes journeyed out from Skipton. Early in the present century Edmond Boggs and his artists explored and revealed the byways of Wharfedale; and in 1902 the railway came to Grassington. What the 'day excursion ticket' began, bus, coach and motor car have completed. Today, caravan, camp-site, and the 'weekend cottage' have brought a more permanent element of the outside world, and make a significant contribution to the economy of the dale.

Roads up-dale converge at Kettlewell, where The Bluebell (A.D. 1680) and The Racehorses – the latter an enlarged Georgian inn dating from 1740 – face each other by the bridge over Cam Beck, which divides the village. Though there is some doubt as to the origin of its name, which may mean a 'stream in the valley' or 'Ketel's spring', there has never been any doubt about the importance of its position, for it lay on a Roman road from Bainbridge to Ilkley, and on the monastic way from Coverham Abbey, which along with Bolton and Fountains held possessions here. This same route from Coverdale was also used for a while on the Skipton to Richmond run in coaching days, but proved too difficult. Those who make the journey by the modern metalled road will appreciate the past hazards of the Park Rash Pass to Coverdale, with its elbow bends and 1 in 4 gradient. From the head of the valley over Fleet Moss once came travellers, pedlars and packmen, along the route from Wensleydale and Scotland. Kettlewell's markets, which fell into decline after the dis-afforestation of the early seventeenth century, and its smithies, must have been very busy places, in the days of horse travel. In addition to catering for horses, the smith also shod cattle and maintained farm and mining equipment. Today, the black-smith is less pressed; a notice on the door of the forge by the bridge reads: "For shoeing appointments, please phone . . ."

One man who has good reason to know the roads of the dale is Jim Wiseman, now retired, who still lives by the Wharfe in the cottage where he was born, and whose family came from Swaledale in the mid-eighteenth century, "wit' miners who were sent to oppen t'Kettlewell mines out". His father, well known as a carrier, took away the last load of lead from the Providence Mine on Great Whernside, and carried all manner of goods – timber, groceries, and dalesfolks' shopping orders – between Skipton and the dalehead. Jim spoke of "t'owd folk" of the valley – the Fosters and the Beresfords of Langstrothdale – and clearly remembered the fairs, down to the very dates – the Lamb Fair (2 September), the Hiring Fair (6 July), when Irishmen gathered for haytime ("it was a big day 'ere, was that!"), and T'owd Yow (Ewe) Fair (23 October) ("It was a busy place then, was Kettlewell, ya know!").

The village was certainly a busy place in the first half of the nineteenth century, with inns, schools, shoemakers, lead-mining, and cotton spinning and weaving. At the end of a shady lane opposite the post office traces of the old mill dam

Winter in Littondale

Kilnsey Hall

Owlcotes, Littondale

Arncliffe church, Littondale

River Skirfare, near Litton

Coverham Abbey
Above south arcade;
Right effigies

Oughtershaw, Wharfedale

Hubberholme church

Penyghent from Winskill

Penyghent Gill

Drystone wall enclosures near Malham Tarn

Iron Age hutment near Penyghent, Ribblesdale

Feizor, near Settle

Celtic wall, Smearsett

can still be seen in a field by the beck. A grassy embankment runs back to houses, and there are more cottages on the opposite bank where looms once operated. This is still a busy corner, in summer, where The King's Head overlooks the old market-place, and the dipper, never at a loss for words, sings in August in the shadows under the bridge. By the parapet, stone steps lead down to the water's edge; there are more along the main street, giving access to the stream from which village folk formerly took water, and cattle drank.

Round the corner an eighty-year-old maypole has been re-erected under the auspices of the Women's Institute, and in the Garden of Remembrance nearby, unnoticed among roses in summer, are the moss-grown uprights of the village stocks.

Kettlewell is dominated by the high mass of Great Whernside (2,310 feet) and by the outliers of Buckden Pike (2,302 feet) – Tor Mere Top and Cam Head. Those who wish to leave Wharfedale for Coverdale at this stage of the journey can do so by Park Rash, a steep and tortuous climb through the fifteenth-century deer park of Ralph, Earl of Westmorland, which ends at the final escarpment. Beneath the limestone crag, and extending for a mile or so on each side of the road, an entrenchment known as Tor Dyke may mark the northern limits of Scale Park, or have its origins as a defensive ditch of Romano-British date, linked, perhaps, with Brigantian fortifications on Ingleborough. It is best seen from the summit of the pass; close by, the old market track from Starbotton heads for Nidderdale, climbing over the col between Great and Little Whernside (1,984 feet), and passing within sight of the monastic landmark of Hunter's Stone. It is usually a wild and gloomy prospect of boggy fellside, relieved here and there by lighter outcrops of limestone, and with innumerable rills draining down to Park Gill Beck. In one of them, below East Scale Park, Dow Cave attracts many younger enthusiasts.

By this route from Kettlewell, two of the National Park's loveliest dales, Wharfedale and Wensleydale, are linked by a third whose appeal lies in a prolonged and sterner grandeur. For almost twelve miles the River Cover, born in the shadow of the Whernsides, descends to join the Yore near Middleham, watering a dale which, like so many others, has in the past century seen a steady decline in population. The sequence is a familiar one – the closure of mine and quarry; the abandoning of old routes and forms of transport; hamlets dwindling to single houses, and houses to dereliction. And in the villages at the foot of the dale, where access is easier, the arrival of the bull's-eye window, the two-car garage, the caravan, and the studio.

A modern tarmac road, much be-gated, follows the traditional route between Wensleydale and the south. Coach and pack horse have followed this track by Hunter's Stone, descending the valley of the Cover towards Middleham. Along the upper dale – the 'High Dale' – hamlets are spaced evenly: Hunter's Hall (or Coverhead) at the river crossing; Woodale; and Bradley, where once an inn lay at the end of the track from Walden, over Dovescar. Horse House is appropriately named, for here pack horses were 'baited' on their journey by a wild track from Arkleside to Nidderdale, over the shoulder of Dead Man's Hill. The hill takes its name from the suspected murders of pedlars at a lonely inn at Lodge, kept by a woman and her daughter. Certainly three headless bodies were discovered in 1728, presumably victims of the deplorable landlady.

A Wesleyan chapel, and in summer the screaming of swifts, heralds the approach to Horse House. Opposite the tiny post office a fine chestnut and a weeping beech almost hide St Botolph's church, with an inevitable tangle of graveyard, and a swallow's nest inside the porch. There a declaration made on the enclosure of Arkleside Common in 1884 ensures the local folk the "privilege of enjoying at all times air, exercise, and recreation" on enclosed land except arable. There are some twenty houses in the village, occupied mostly by 'off-comers'. Once there were two inns, and stables; an existing one, The Thwaite Arms, is dated 1888. A laconic notice outside announces "Food"; and by the village store, another: "Last shop for eight miles".

Between walls and hedges the narrow road winds down the dale, which begins to widen between Harland Hill (1,758 feet) and Great Haw (1,786 feet). The hamlet of Gammersgill lies among trees, and is reduced to two families. A private road up Flemmis Gill leads to Fleensop. At Hall Farm, dated '1737 G R', John Bostock keeps a flock of three hundred Dales-bred lambing ewes, which apart from being brought in "t't'tup" in November, are kept on the fell as long as possible throughout

the year. If winters are very severe, the flock is taken down for
hay and concentrates. "But," John told me, "thi' do better on t'
moor if ye can git hay to 'em. Thi' scratch in t' moss-bobs
[heather]. Then wi can save t' inside land for lambing-time."
It is often mid May before the cattle get their turn outdoors.
John has his flock on gated land on Gammersgill Moor
adjoining Walden, but maintains that the best summer land
for sheep is up at Coverhead, "on t' limestone". In mid July
you may come upon a scene of activity at Hale Farm, as
hoggetts are brought into the yard for their first shearing. A
large sheet is spread out in the yard, jackets come off, and a
wall-eyed sheep-dog prostrates itself in the shade of a
sycamore, panting. You will meet John's helper, Jack Yeoman
– "Jack ere's 'ad 'is feet i'Coverd'l' all 'is life!" The fleeces are
deftly rolled and tied, and stacked on the sheet by a lad.
Presently they will be collected and taken to the factory at
Bradford, where they will be graded and weighed. I asked
about weight and prices. "A good 'un 'll fitch twenty-five
bob," Jack told me, "but thi' weigh in kilos now, and ah doan't
understan' that sort a' thing," In Coverdale the E.E.C. is not
the most popular of topics!

Beyond Gammersgill the road down-dale, with its views of
Roova Crags and Flamstone Pin, turns sharply into Carlton,
once a headquarters of the forest; courts were held in the Hall
Cote. In the long high street with its eighteenth-century houses
one can stop by The Forester's Arms, and in a lane behind the
inn, can note the green mound surmounted by trees, variously
described as a Bronze Age tumulus, a Norman motte, and the
site of an ancient parliament; perhaps it has served all three
functions. Visitors turning into the village from the west may
notice an empty house with a padlocked door that stands
forlornly behind its little patch of garden. Here lived and
worked the remarkable family of Binks – three generations of
cobblers, each called Christopher, whose work was renowned
beyond the limits of Coverdale. The third Christopher, who
died in 1973 at the age of eighty-two retired only a few years
before his death. Like his father and grandfather before him he
travelled throughout the dale selling his goods. The cobblers
were well known also in Nidderdale to which they travelled
with their packs by way of Arkleside and Dead Man's Hill.
The last Christopher, always thrifty, adapted a bicycle to carry

his wares, which were accommodated in a large Gladstone bag strapped to a carrier. History does not record how he performed the Herculean task of ascending the steep and rough tracks of Arkleside with such an encumbrance. Christopher's wife Jane Ann, who came from nearby Melmerby over eighty years ago, and who still lives in Carlton, recalled for me the journeyings of her late husband. "'E wouldn't spend his munny, and buy a car; all 'e 'ad was 'is owd bike. Offen as not 'e was as wet as a sieve," she told me. "One day 'e wur caught i' snow cumin' over fra' Nidd'd'le, and if it 'adn't bin fer lights i' Arkleside i'd nivver 'a' got 'ome!"

Farmers and gamekeepers valued Binks' boots highly for the excellence of their workmanship; often two pairs were bought at once by farmers, who used to hang up one pair for a year or so to season. Shoes, made with their own tools, wax and dyes, took a fortnight to make, and boots, three weeks. Their ledger for 1898 includes an item, "To Ramshaw Robinson of Carlton – boots soled and heeled 4/6d [23p]." In 1899 a pair of "Belst" (best?) boots cost 18/6d (92½p).

Methodism has always had a strong footing in Coverdale, and Jane Ann Binks remembers early meetings held in cottages, describing her first introduction to the new chapel at 'Melby' (Melmerby) and 'Sunda' Skule' as the biggest influences in her life. The annual procession of witness, or 'Love Feasts', are still held in June to celebrate 'John Wesley day'. "But," says Jane Ann, "thi' not the same as thi' used to be. Ah've seen places pack'd to t'door; nowbody would 'a' missed."

After morning service and the Sacrament, dalesfolk made their testimony: "The devil had me hedged in on all sides, I could not get out no-how until I remembered there was a way out at t'top; my friend the devil's a good hedger, but he's a rotten thatcher."

Roads from Carlton pass over the flanks of Penhill to Wensleydale, but the visitor who follows them directly will in doing so miss the delights of the final reaches of the Cover, which add a glimpse of history.

Half a mile south of Carlton, a narrow lane winds down to the river. In summer, sweet cicely and jack-by-the-hedge exchange amorous glances across the flowery way to West Scrafton, and greenfinches wax eloquent at the unexpected wealth of hedgerows in this secret corner of the Dales. The village, deceptively large, has retained its character better than most. Houses stand round a small green, though some appear to have turned their back upon it. There is an air of eccentricity about their varied and curiously pitched roofs; outhouses, barns, and out-shutts extend in all directions. One house, formerly an inn in the days of mining and quarrying, has a singularly tall chimney stack. In the warm light of the autumn day when I last visited the village, the beautifully coloured cottages of Coverdale sandstone took on the hint of honey against their background of purple moorland. Outside a barn at Garth House farm a pile of bracken, newly gathered for winter bedding, added its own warmth of colour. I exchanged the time of day with an old man in shirt sleeves, rebuilding his garden wall.

"Ah've bin rootin' at it now fer two hours, and ah 'aven't got it bedded yit," he told me, without pausing in his task.

A sunflower inclined its exotic head from the cottage wall, watching in silence, and two coloured butterflies, bent on their own business, paid court to his Michaelmas daisies. For man and red admiral there is a sense of urgency in late September that is understandable, for this hollow beneath the crags is soon in shadow when the sun begins to dip early behind enclosing hills. This is the 'money' side of the dale. Around the corner beyond Eastfield Farm a sudden long view of Penhill, still in sunshine, presently revealed the 'sunny' side.

In the confines of the lower dale antiquity has left a generous legacy. There are glimpses of Carlton, with its ancient mounds and strip cultivation, on the opposite bank at Cotescue, the remains of a fifteenth-century deer park; at the river, a pack-horse bridge and the site of St Simon's chapel founded in 1328. This was first occupied by a hermit, and after the Dissolution, by a publican who converted the building to an ale house. The hamlet of Caldbergh stands aloof and elevated above the Cover, now only a voice in this densely wooded section of the dale. Here, or hereabouts, is the reputed birthplace of Miles Coverdale, scholar and priest, who in 1535 first translated the Bible into English. In 1538 Henry VIII ordered that "one book of the whole Bible in English in the Largest volume" should be provided for every church, and Coverdale was responsible for the publication in 1539 of this 'Great Bible'. On the south side of the river the spoil heaps of lead and coal mining scar the hillside of Flamstone Pin, and at Castle Steads and in Red Beck Gill are the earthworks of Iron Age forts. Below them a National Trust sign introduces Braithwaite Hall, a grey, three-gabled, high-chimneyed manor house, once a grange of Jervaulx Abbey, and now noted for its oak staircase, floors, and eighteenth-century panelling. The road now passes to the race-horse country of Middleham, by way of East Witton, where two orderly lines of houses, regularly spaced and with low pitched roofs, flank a strip of green. There is something almost modern in the uniformity of the houses, which along with the church were built in the first years of the nineteenth century by the Marquess of Ailesbury, who thus remodelled a village which had suffered fire and plague, and the re-routing of the main road. In the adjoining hamlet of Lowthorpe, beyond a handsome farmstead with tiled roofs, the old burial ground lies among trees – a place of shadows and desolation, where drunken gravestones and gaping table tombs tilt in the grip of gnarled beech roots, and nettles obscure the merits of those who have lain there for almost three centuries. Of the old church there is no trace, its stones were used in the building of houses, and of the new church in 1809, at the Jubilee of George III. In East Witton the dalesfolk are obviously conscious of their charming village. Young chestnuts have been planted on the green; hollyhocks stand on guard against the porches hung with honeysuckle; and at one cottage a bisected millstone supports a display of pansies by the garden gate. Folk will point out the taps on the green – one set in a huge erratic of Shap granite removed from the fell above – and will direct you to 'Slaverin' Sal', a watery grotto on the hillside south of the village. It is with reluctance that one turns to retrace one's steps along the Cover; but the most enchanting discoveries have yet to be made.

By Coverham Bridge, with its unusual pointed arch and parapets, a narrow lane passes down beneath the inner gateway to what remains of the medieval glory of the abbey. The Premonstratensian abbey of Coverham, removed from Swainby on the Swale by Ranulph FitzRobert, was built by the Cover in 1212, ultimately housing an abbot and sixteen canons, and employing many local people in its bakehouse, brewery and kitchens. After the Dissolution this lovely resting place for travellers on the route to Lancashire was sadly missed.

The ruins of Coverham, in private grounds, are not on the grand scale of those at Fountains, Jervaulx and Bolton Priory, but the veneration of the centuries, the hand of nature, and the labour and dedication of a sympathetic land-owner have contrived to produce by the Cover a manifestation of that idyllic scenario for which the Pennines are renowned. Yet here is a ruin with a difference, for on this site houses and abbey have become one, and in Mrs Webster's monastery garden it is difficult to tell where past ends and present begins. In March, snowdrops line the drive on the north side, set beneath trees and transept lancets. Through an iron gate there are glimpses of a garden graced with the piers of two arches, once part of the south arcade. Fragments of sculpture and monastic plaques are embodied in the house walls. A room with a fine transomed window with nine lights was originally the sixteenth-century gatehouse. Stone coffins and a high altar, bright with flowers, mark the chancel. In the yard at the rear, stone effigies, reputedly of Ranulph FitzRobert and his son, are set against a wall. There are mouldings, gargoyles and tablets. In October when valerian festoons the stonework, and the debris of autumn gathers in every nook and cranny, the thin dirge of the robin sounds the passing of yet another summer over this wistful corner of Coverham.

Contemporary with the abbey, though heavily restored subsequently, the thirteenth-century church of the Holy Trinity stands nearby in a wooded churchyard above the river, with seemingly few of the rustic graces of, say, Arncliffe or Hubberholme. Perhaps it languished too long in the shadow of the abbey; perhaps the presence of Scots pines in a graveyard that descends from an overgrown corner to a lower level does little to help. Here, out of sight of the church, the sound of water passing down a former mill race of stone supposedly drowns the sound of the bells. Below, an old mill built by the monks, and a house, once the home of the miller, lie by the riverside where once the white-robed custodians greeted travellers at the abbey gate and the acolyte received gifts by St Simon's ford. There can be few places where it is easier to dream away the centuries than in the leafy recesses of Coverham.

A journey down the Cover takes one many miles from Wharfedale, and with Middleham and Jervaulx ahead it is unlikely that the visitor will want to forgo the more immediate attractions of Wensleydale - Penhill, West Burton, Walden and Aysgarth. Those with a mind for ecclesiastical architecture may wish to travel down by Masham to Ripon and Fountains Abbey. In any event, the return to Kettlewell by Bishopdale offers an easier route than the gated one by Coverdale, at the end of a long journey of discovery. The delights of upper Wharfedale can best be enjoyed on another day.

One of the most entrancing views of Wharfedale is that from the edge of the limestone terrace of Knipe Scar, along the track from Arncliffe and Hawkswick by Old Cote Moor. Grass Wood, where the Wharfe emerges from woodland, and the buttress of Kilnsey Crag, dominate to the south, and the concentration of lynchets on the approaches to Kettlewell are seen to advantage. In summer, these rocky heights and their abundant cover of ash trees are pleasantly cool. Parties of jackdaws exercise their young in the upward currents, and kestrels hang above the scarp, as if stationed regularly to guard the way updale. In July, in clearings along the scree, one can look for the gorgeous bloody cranesbill, or listen to the re-iterated chant of the redstart. On the edge of the moor, tracks run in all directions. Some are sheep-trods, but broader ones are clearly those of man.

Old market routes between Ribblesdale and Wensleydale can still be traced from Settle to Askrigg, Aysgarth, and Masham. They survive as grass tracks, modern roads, or bridle paths, like the one that passes eastward over the moor here to Wharfedale. This route crossed the river, and climbed to Cam Head by way of Starbotton, where it is now seen as a walled track - one of two that rear up sharply on each side of Cam Gill beck. Starbotton village, the last up-dale to be mentioned in the Domesday Survey, is a wonderfully compact collection of seventeenth- and eighteenth-century houses, many of the latter smaller and neater, a legacy of the lead-mining era. Today, another element is visible, that of clean-stoned current restoration, and some newer building: of thirty-six houses, half are owned by weekenders and off-comers. Even the school has been converted.

One of the most impressive houses, standing in a back lane

against the fellside, is the old hall, where in July 1667 the ageing Lady Anne Clifford, on her way to Pendragon Castle, stayed overnight; her host was John Symondson. The hall, now three cottages, bears three different datestones, but some doubt has been cast on the authenticity of two of them, which may have been added later during alterations. The one thought to be genuine heads the doorway at the western end, and reads 'W S 1663 T S'. Next door but one, at 'Wellside', lives septuagenarian Norman ('Dan' to his friends) Parrington, gardener, waller, and general factotem. No one would call Dan a historian – "Lady Anne Clifford? Bit before my time!" But I found him a mine of information on drystone walling. He explained the niceties of 'batter', 'through stones', and 'cap-stones'. "Wi call 'em ceapin stones, or topst'n's i' Wharfed'le," he explained. "Ya mun cross ivvry joint, too." Dan pointed out the site of the smelt mill along the beck, the ruined chimney, and the old workings, where only recently potholers had unearthed a human skeleton – "It wer all bones an' buttons!" Dan went back to his wheelbarrow. I jokingly suggested that it was time he retired. "Oh 'ell!" he bristled. "Ah'm seventy-fower now, an' ah'm busier than ah've ivver bin; ah nivver stop." There are many 'owd 'uns' in the dale who have never learnt to stop. Perhaps the valley was a healthier place when Dan attended school at Buckden. Or perhaps it was that the unhealthy ones went early to the churchyard.

As Semerwater has its stories of a sunken city, so Starbotton must come close to having its own legend, for how it has survived the centuries without being swallowed up by the hills is a mystery. As one climbs the stony track of the Old Road to Cam Head the enclosed nature of the village becomes in-creasingly apparent. Clustered among trees, its roof-tops sag, as if the weight of the hills were upon them, defenceless in the very jaws of the gill. On more than one occasion the beck has sought to do what the hills could not, bursting its banks to engulf the hamlet. In 1686 the devastation was almost com-plete; bridges were washed away, and houses destroyed.

Above the village, on the edge of the gill, a derelict smelt mill chimney, crenellated by time, fights a losing battle with the years. From its walled base a diagonal line of rubble, once the flue, ends by the beck on a stony clearing, which is all that remains of the mill itself. The squared chimney was clearly a substantial structure, far more so than would seem necessary for the much smaller bore of the flue.

At the beginning of September there appear those subtle changes in the Dales landscape that mark the beginning of a long and gradual decline into winter. This is especially notice-able on grassland. On limestone, the hills gradually assume an olive green after the seeding of sheep's fescue and blue moor grass, before passing to the duller olive of winter. Paradoxically, rain and sun in September often bring a renewed emerald reminiscent of springtime to bottom land. On shales and gritstone, mat-grass bleaches to the palest buff, while fells of molinia and cotton sedge undergo an intensification of buff and russet, colouring progressively to reach a climax towards the end of November. This reciprocal loss and heightening of colour of clowder and moortop is particularly noticeable where calcareous and acid soils lie in close proximity, as at the head of Wharfedale.

Sitting near the smelt mill chimney above Starbotton in early September one senses these imperceptible signs of the changing season; white mushroom discs and seeding thistles; tortoiseshell butterfly taken by the wind; ripening fruit on the rowan. Only the ash trees keep faith, with foliage of changeless hue till the last leaf is cast. Cam Gill is not the best wooded of valleys, and its flexed shoulders, smooth and bare, muscle down towards the village. From a vantage point nearby, one can pick out the old hall (a doll's house); The Fox and Hounds (with its walnut tree outside, and old Dan inside); and beyond the main road, the enclosed Quaker burial-ground (now contain-ing more sheep and hens than Quakers). On the far slope, a monotone of green is the scarp of Fosse Wood, and from its base long lines of walling descend to divide the meadowland evenly into strips with access to water.

From Hubberholme to Kettlewell the Wharfe wanders at will along its fertile flood plain, as if to enjoy its first taste of freedom in an idyll of willows, buttercup fields, and black and white cattle that contemplate summer from its pleasant shallows. Beneath high banks, where the river dreams its way through tunnels of shadow, and trout lie deep, the kingfisher plummets from his perch, shattering for a moment the image of summer. His nesting hole in the bank may be distinguished from that of the sandmartin by its vertical oval, and, as the young grow, by the tell-tale droppings that exude from its entrance. The kingfisher is normally associated with slower reaches of river where fish lie but just beneath the surface in still pools, for this bird, unlike the dipper, must first mark down his prey from above, before diving. From Kettlewell to Buckden the birds' shrill call, often a multiple note near the nest, is a familiar sound.

Buckden, established as a forest headquarters in Norman times under the lordship of the Percys, lies on the edge of Langstrothdale Chase. Its name suggests its ancient disposition, a reference also preserved in the name and sign of The Buck Inn which stands back from the road. The wild roe deer by which the feudal lords set so much store are, of course, long gone. So too is the emparked herd of fallow deer which so delighted Miss Pontefract. Elevated above the river, the village still has its by-ways, unseen from the road, that run back up the slopes of Buckden Pike, though many of the houses, remodelled to suit the needs of townsfolk, have lost much of their appeal. Indeed, the approaches from Kettlewell are completely changed in character, and Buckden, like so many other villages, has been restyled to cater for the growing number of visitors who pass through this Dales junction. Its snack bar, craft shop, and holiday accommodation are quite predictable, and one must allow that its discreetly sited car park is an advance on that of Kettlewell. It still requires a great stretch of the imagination to picture Buckden in the days when Tom Airey's mail coach from Grassington used to arrive by The Buck, and the autumn fairs and feasts were celebrated with dancing and donkey rides.

There are some affinities between this village and Starbotton. Each is dominated by the mass of Buckden Pike, and lies at the foot of a narrow gill with waterfalls and remains of lead mining. But at Starbotton the tourist usually passes through, whereas Buckden is a natural stopping place. Here one pauses for refreshment; surveys the wooded prospect where the Wharfe bends into Langstrothdale; makes the ascent of Buckden Pike; or follows the track by Rakes Wood, along the course of the Roman road to Bainbridge. This looks down on the hamlet of Cray. Seventy years ago the then landlord of the local was remembered by Willie Foster in his 'Song of Upper Wharfedale'.

'Ben Lofthouse loves Cray and his White Lion Inn,
While his grand trotting horse the prizes does win'.

Whatever else its attributes, Ben's horse certainly never trotted up the steep hill to Kidstones Pass, where it is joined by a natural terrace that carries the track from the Rakes. This route to Bishopdale and Wensleydale is arguably the finest manifestation of the scenic qualities of the Yoredales, whose stepped terraces of limestone here form an amphitheatre. For a few hours after heavy rain these take on the effect of a grand water spectacle, with innumerable cascades at work – a fitting finale for those who leave the Wharfe at Buckden.

For a brief spell there are two roads up-dale, one on each side of the river before its final reaches into Langstrothdale. The valley bends, and woodland clothes its sides; in October, a mile or so of colour enhances the way to Raisgill. Though ash trees still predominate, there is a fair admixture of sycamore and birch; trees on the hillside, and overhanging a river of changing character, for now the Wharfe romps down in mirthful spasms over outcrop, pavement, and shingle. At Hubberholme there are usually more stones than water, and visitors gather by the bridge, or discover the delightful parish church, squat of tower, grey and venerable, and scarcely visible among dark yews. There are few more impressive interiors than that of St Michael and All Angels. A rough stone arcade of arches, possibly twelfth century, iron candelabra, a pulpit dated 1641 and a magnificent oak rood loft with the Percy badge dated 1558, give a touch of the medieval. More recent work is seen in the pews, stalls and chairs, which bear the sign of the 'Mouse-man' – the work of Thompson of Kilburn, in 1934. Originally a forest chapel, 'Hub'ram' was given by William de Percy to the monks of Coverham Abbey in 1241. After the Dissolution in 1539 it became a chapel of ease on Arncliffe and was served by the curates of Halton Gill. One of these, Miles Wilson, who had to make the hazardous journey by way of the 2,000-foot Horse-head Pass from Littondale, wrote in 1743: 'in the winter quarter it is with great danger and difficulty I pass over very high mountain and large drifts of snow to the chapel'. A Mr Lindley, a subsequent curate of Halton Gill, took services at Hubberholme for over thirty years; latterly, as an old man, he made the journey over the hill on horseback. The distant sighting of his white horse was the signal for the bellringer to begin his task. Panels in the Lewis window, in the south-east corner of the church, commemorate these intrepid curates. Across the bridge at The George Inn, once residence of the vicar, the 'Hubberholme Parliament' still meets annually for 'land-letting', perpetuating an ancient charity. The disposal of the sixteen-acre field nearby, described by one dalesman as "nowt but a lump a' stoan", is held on a day in January. To escape an invasion by tourists, the date is now unspecified.

Within the old Forest of Langstroth, marked near Buckden with a stone 'cross', a stern beauty pervades the head of the dale, and one can speculate on its wildness in the days when the Normans imposed their rigorous forest laws on this overgrown upland to ensure the preservation of game and deer. Existing settlements were absorbed and many became forest lodges. As might be expected, names of Norse derivation are common: Hubberholme; Raisgill, where a bridle path climbs to the summit of Horsehead Pass for Littondale; Yockenthwaite; 'Eogan's Clearing', with its beautiful pack-horse bridge. To the west of the hamlet on the north bank of the river a rough circle of stones marks a Bronze Age site, probably a burial mound; at Deepdale, at the foot of a gill are the remains of Iron Age enclosures.

In medieval times Langstrothdale Chase was sacrosanct; currently, throughout summer, it is Everybody's Dale. A wet spell in early autumn may deter many visitors. On a September morning in the rain it is very green along the river above Hubberholme. Rambler roses still bloom on the shady walls of the farm at Raisgill, where bracken is beginning to turn. At midday, a Post Office van trundles over the narrow bridge at Yockenthwaite; sheep have sought the shelter of walls; and one or two picnic parties sit by the river in cars, and watch the water rise and turn to ginger wine. A rising wind tunes the instrument of the sycamores elevated at Deepdale, and they respond with a roar; Scots pines hiss continuously; holly has a dry and brittle sound; and the ashes overhanging the Wharfe, less strident than broad-leaved trees, sing with a pleasing treble. Road and river, and the music of wind and water, are in harmony beyond Deepdale; there is much to be said for a rainy day in Wharfedale.

Beckermonds, where Greenfield and Oughtershaw Becks

unite to become the Wharfe, was once the centre of activities
in the upper dale. Here lived two remarkable families, the
Fosters, and their relatives, the Beresfords of Yockenthwaite.
Between them, they made the dale a lively place at the turn of
the century. At 'Beckermonds Ball' the 'Langstrothdale String
Band' played for dancing, and on Guy Fawkes Night bonfires
were held on Harpot Green, below the bridge. Music was a
feature of every social occasion. Willie Foster was sometimes
joined on concertina by Alan Beresford, who also performed a
simultaneous reel. The dale had its own special dances, like
'Buttered Peas' and 'Huntsman's Chorus'. The local dalesmen
were enthusiastic hunters, especially in the case of one particular otter which evaded pursuit throughout the winter of
1901:

Next, Banks and Turnbull had him in Harpot beneath the ice,
For half a day they watched like cats watch mice,
But he was in a hole not far away,
Jack Beresford had traced him that day
He went that neet.

The last great celebration at Beckermonds was held for the
Coronation of King George V, with sports and dancing. A
marquee was erected, and decorated with flowers, and a brass
band travelled nine miles from Hardraw, over Fleet Moss,
With the First World War came the end of an era. Hannah
and William Foster, the parents of ten children, rest in the
churchyard at Hubberholme. It is many a long day since Jack
Foster cut peat on Deepdale Fell, and scythed hay right down
to the river in Greenfield, with muslin over his head to keep off
midges. For fully seventy years the ash tree has spread its
growing canopy over the bridge at Beckermonds; seventy times
the sandpiper has returned to the beck. In the meantime, the
grim reaper has done some cutting of his own in the meadows
of the dale head, and the name of Foster is only a memory at
Beckermonds. At the mouth of Oughtershaw Beck two well-
appointed houses behind white paddock rails and a 'Private'
notice look across to the little bridge that once knew the boat,
the bonfire, and *bonhomie* of a more sociable era. On the wet
blustery September day when I came to Beckermonds a wild
wind was at work in the copse, and a frenzy of captive leaves
swirled madly in the confines of the lane. A few dejected geese

sat hunched in the lee of a wall, and a little way down the track the grey rambling old home of the Fosters, a curiously cramped building, enlarged to meet the needs of a growing family and hired helps, straddled the road to Greenfield. Red paintwork and orange marigolds – a good old English flower – did their best to brighten the house, now the home of a good old English daleswoman called Margaret, who, without the slightest inhibition, revealed her age as being between fifty and a hundred.

"Ah wuz a Turnbull, but now ah'm a Mudd!" she told me.

I remembered Willies Foster's poem;

Turnbull is next, and he keeps a shop;
Nothing he's short of from needle to pop.

Margaret required little prompting to recall her childhood, and her school days with the Fosters at Oughtershaw. In her abrupt way she recited the names of them all.

"Thi' wur grand scholars; ten o' them, and nine of us Turnbulls."

She directed me to the farm outbuildings. One is dated 'RS 1674'. Next to "t'owd building" two derelict round-headed doors hung with mole traps open into a barn with an upper storey, where the 'String Band' used to play for dancing – "Butt'd Poys, Shottish, and t'Lancers".

A few minutes later the postman arrived – with the morning paper. I took my leave of Margaret Mudd: "Thur's no pleace like Beggarman's to moy. Wi'v lived eyer i' Groenv'l'd twenty-eight years, an' ail, rain, snow and blow, ah've luv'd it. Thur's nobbut us and mi bruther – only about fower; rest's new 'uns. I like t'owd uns!"

The wind ruffled the fleeces of a flock of sheep awaiting dipping, and tossed the restless swallows. As I left a heavy waggon churned up the mud of Beckermonds, and with a load of clean fence posts for the new plantations of the Economic Forestry Group, headed up the gated road to 'Grenefield Coshe'. I thought of Ninian and Jeff of High Greenfield, who once shot pigeons on a fellside now submerged in conifers; and Margaret Mudd's obituary seemed particularly poignant – it is a not unfamiliar theme in these dales.

The road that climbs gently to Oughtershaw gives little idea of the ascent that is to follow, nor did it on that wild grey day in any way dispel the impression of melancholy. The Hall, built in 1849 by the Woodd family, lies behind double gates and walls in a narrow belt of parkland squeezed into a wooded ravine. The Victorian church-cum-school, now defunct, has all the accoutrements of a classical temple, a ponderous neo-Corinthian memento of a departed age, bearing in the form of a plaque mute testimony to a family tragedy. The nearby hamlet of Oughtershaw, grimly uncompromising in the elements, makes few concessions to civilization apart from a telephone box. A pile of newly cut logs is freshly stacked for winter, and a protracted line of farm machinery, ancient and modern, points the way to the hills, but not, apparently, to bankruptcy. As the road begins to rise between walls hung with white stonecrop there are visions of ash trees flailing the wind from rocky plinths, and lonely barns whose roof-trees sag as with the weight of the years. Through a window in the veil of drifting cloud the saturnine curve of Ingleborough rises out of Greenfield head, and beyond Nethergill and Swarthgill the valley bottom, abandoned apparently to the mercies of the moor, suddenly blossoms again beneath the solitudes of Cam Houses. "If it is true that every house is haunted where men have lived ... it is just as true ... of the dark tracks they followed when storm witches rode out from the north east", wrote Halliwell Sutcliffe. There are dark tracks enough at the head of Langstrothdale, and the shells of houses forgotten now under a blanket of firs. The Romans knew the Cam Road from Bainbridge, and old tracks led from Ribblesdale to Littondale, Wharfedale and Wensleydale. If the spirits of the departed still linger anywhere it is in those unfathomable acres above Cam Houses, where, it is said, a man once sold his wife for five gold sovereigns and a cart of peat, and where a spectral white dog may run with you over Yorkshire's highest road. Or, deliberating at the time-worn crossroad above Cam, you may find the spirit of Jerry at your elbow to help you make up your mind. But these are of small account. As Richard Jefferies discovered, ghosts die as we grow older, and their places are taken by real ghosts. There are many of them – Fosters, Beresfords, Turnbulls, Peacocks, Calverts – on the heights above Oughtershaw and 'Dib'd'le; for the dark Valkyries are never absent for long from the misty wastes of Fleet Moss.

The Wharfe, as Oughtershaw Beck, rises on the southern

flanks of Dodd Fell (2,185 feet) on the watershed which also gives birth to Cam Beck, a main tributary of the Ribble. For a mile or so at the summit of the pass the road traverses this level ridge, from which there are views of the heads of Raydale, Bardale and Sleddale. Addlebrough rises squarely to the north-east, and if you stand on tiptoe, as it were, you will see Semerwater. Affinities are now towards Wensleydale, and it is a choice between the rival claims of golden plover on the hags of Dodd Fell, or poached eggs on toast at Hawes.

IV

THE HEART OF CRAVEN

IT IS NOT SURPRISING that the town of Skipton, lying as it does on a traditional trade route across the Pennines, has been called a 'Gateway to the Dales', for road, rail, and canal come to it. Day and overnight visitors throng its shops and cafes, stalls line the main street, and its parish church looks down each day on a stream of traffic moving steadily to right and left to follow the valleys of Wharfe, Aire or Ribble. At this point only a few miles separate the roughly parallel courses of the three rivers, but the Aire is a minor stream bordered by the drumlin field which at the end of the glacial epoch captured and diverted its headwaters, turning them westward into the Ribble. Today the road from Gargrave to Hellifield, or from Skipton to Gisburn, meanders and undulates through a 'basket of eggs' landscape; a concentration of rounded hills of clay and debris which were deposited beneath retreating ice, and which now provide a watershed between the Aire and Ribble.

Skipton itself is a glorious mixture of past and present, a go-ahead little town of comings and goings. Its name derives from 'Sheeptown', and cattle and sheep are still very much a part of its life, but with an overlay of hi-fi and bingo, art galleries and fashionable shops. Here culture and commerce go hand in hand; it has the best fish and chips outside Lancashire, and a Chinese restaurant that serves bamboo shoots and Yorkshire pudding (not together!). On Chapel Hill a thirteenth-century cornmill worked by water from Eller Beck has been restored, and can be seen driving machinery, and millstones. In the Craven Museum is exhibited an interesting collection of early artifacts, geological specimens, and mining tools, of special appeal to those on tour in the district. The parish church, standing at the head of High Street, has an oak roof and a sixteenth-century rood screen. Close to the church, the massive gateway of Skipton Castle, embellished with the motto 'Desormais' (Henceforth), gives access to the fortress-palace of the Cliffords, erected in 1311 on the site of a Norman

keep built by Robert de Romille. Following the Civil War the
castle was restored by the Lady Anne Clifford, who also erected
the heraldic table tomb to the memory of her father in the
parish church. Students of history will find many references to
this pious and persistent gentlewoman. Considering that she
was in her fifties before she came to her northern estates, Lady
Anne certainly left her mark upon the Dales, particularly those
that lay along her route northward, following Wharfe, Ure,
Lune or Eden to her castle at Brougham. At almost every stage
there is some reminder of her presence – building, road, or
memorial. In fact, one might go so far as to refer to the Lady
Anne Clifford as the second most illustrious name in dales
history; the first, as they will tell you in Skipton, will always be
that of 'Fiery Fred' Trueman whose story is, unfortunately, less
relevant to these chronicles!

Those who sail the waters of the Leeds and Liverpool Canal
which here descends after its crossing of the Pennines, will
know Gargrave for its locks and pleasant halting places. The
village, which lies between the canal and the Aire in a fertile
countryside of woods and parkland, had in monastic times
connections with the abbey of Sawley, in Ribblesdale. The
remains of crosses of Anglo-Danish origin on the north porch
of the church provide evidence of a much earlier pre-Conquest
building. Parishes then were extensive, this one extending some
ten or fifteen miles into Ribblesdale, and towards Malham,
through an area whose settlement was mainly Anglian –
Hetton, Eshton, Calton, and Malham. The Danish element is
seen in the names of Flasby and Kirkby Malham. Narrow
winding lanes traverse this countryside, and walkers can follow
the Pennine Way along the banks of the Aire.

Eshton Hall, once the home of the Wilsons and now a
nursing-home, is set in fine parkland with plantations of
thicker woodland. Here the beck sparkles beneath the bridge
that leads to Wharfedale, overhung with stately beeches – a
colourful corner in autumn when pheasants come out from
cover, and giant hogweed stands eight feet high by the streamside. The time to see Eshton is, however, in early spring when
the woodland path is a white carpet of snowdrops, and beech
and ash boles sustain their delicate tracery against a March sky
freshly blue. Some felling has recently taken place, and on one
occasion I came across a woodman cutting and bagging logs in

a sheltered corner. As I left he apologetically locked the estate gate behind me. "If ah doan't, thi'll walk!" he explained, indicating his huge stack of billets. "Ah lost fotty bags last yeer."

In the miles that lie ahead the church seems to have exercised an unusually strong influence on the lives of the dalesfolk, most of the land formerly being monastic property. Near Winterburn an imposing seventeenth-century house called Friar's Head stands on the site of a grange of Furness Abbey; the hamlet itself was a centre of early Nonconformity at the beginning of the nineteenth century. As in so many dales, Methodism flourished here where poor and hard-working folk from the mines, quarries and farms readily identified themselves with the forthright and democratic way of the chapel, rather than with the established church, which was the prerogative of the upper classes.

On the final stage of its journey towards Malham the road winds and dips into the secluded village of Kirkby Malham. When you have drunk your fill of the sheer beauty of the hamlet in the hollow, seek out the unusual in the churchyard, which has a grave with a stream running through it. In the church of St Michael the Archangel a font that may be Danish was rescued about a century ago from a rubbish heap in the churchyard where it had lain unnoticed. The parish register contains the signature of Oliver Cromwell who in 1655 bore witness to a wedding.

Close to the church two minor roads enter the village. One comes over the flanks of Rye Loaf Hill from Settle and affords fine upland views of Pendle Hill and Ribblesdale; the other, almost overlooked, leads down by Kirkby Beck and crosses the Aire to Hanlith, a cluster of houses on a hillside. The Hall was formerly the home of the Sergeantson family, but has seen much re-styling. The datestone 'R.S. 1668' and original doorway are incorporated in the present building, along with the carving of a halberd on each side of the door jamb. This unusual feature also occurs at New Hall, near Settle, where it denotes the tenure of land as a reward for personal services to a medieval lord.

Those who approach Malham by the time-honoured method of walking may do so by footpath from Hanlith, in which case they will have time to savour the charms of what lies ahead. Indeed, a surprising number of visitors still do arrive in this way, following the last mile (or the first mile, if you prefer) of the Aire along the riverside track, which is a section of the Pennine Way. For others, the narrow road twists up out of Kirkby Malham, and winds between limestone walls, much as it did when early rail excursions brought their waggonettes and sightseers from the train at Skipton, Bell Busk, or Hellifield. But once around the corner, it is a different story. A broad new highway speeds on towards the village, exiles returning after long absence must be prepared for change, particularly around the car park and information centre approaches. This is, of course, a reflection of the times in which we live, and Malham is not peculiar in this respect; it is just that the influx of visitors here is much more than in most dales villages. School parties, family groups and campers throng every nook and corner, and weekends and holidays are scarcely the best time to enjoy the place to the full. In fact, one is inclined to think that if the present trend continues some revision of contour lines by map-makers is going to be necessary! Arriving in the village on a hot June day in Jubilee Year, I found cottages decked with bunting. At one a housewife whose loyalty surpassed her regard for safety was perched on a ladder, nailing a Union Jack to a garden tree, and round the corner a large gathering crowded round the Colne Morris men. Amidst the noise and snarl-up of stationary cars by the bridge two collies and a shepherd were grappling with a flock of sheep bound for the fell. "Gits more like Lundun iv'ry day!" he called out in exasperation as he sweated his way past. The dogs serpentined between car wheels. Exhausts fumed. Laburnum blossom hung. Across the way at an ice-cream kiosk a queue two deep tailed back to The Buck. It's an ill wind ... All of which is not to say that the hills of Malham are completely beyond redemption; in essence, it is the same breath-taking landscape that attracted Gray, the Wordsworths, and Kingsley. The Cove and Gordale have a beauty and tradition unsurpassed in the history of dales landscape, and one would almost wish to have lived two hundred years ago when it was 'discovered'.

To Dorothy and William Wordsworth, who at Gordale "drank of its clear waters", the

chasm, terrific as the lair
Where the young lions crouch

was one of the grandest objects in nature. It was visited by Turner and Girtin and in 1769 Gray's overriding impressions were of horror. In modern times on any summer's day scantily clad schoolchildren in plimsolls may be seen scrambling about its cliffs, over 350 feet high, and no dale has been more walked over, or more fully chronicled, than this one. And yet it may strike one, approaching by way, perhaps, of Airton, that but for a geological accident, the source of the Aire would have been a very orthodox, even minor, topographical feature. The Craven faults, whose effects are seen from Kirkby Lonsdale to Nidderdale, have transformed what would have been a very restrained dale head into a showpiece, for nowhere is the quintessential beauty of limestone more manifest than in the sculptured cliffs, pavements of almost geometrical symmetry, and wayward water courses of Malham and Gordale.

Both of these spectacular features are the result of stream head erosion on the line of the mid-Craven fault, which traverses Kirkby Fell, Pikedaw, and Gordale. To the south of the fault, the landscape is typical of millstone grit county – rough, dark in hue, and with much damp grassland. Northward, Great Scar limestone lies in massive horizontal blocks. At the top end of the Gordale valley, an exposure of smooth grey Silurian slates marks the line of the north Craven fault, visible again at the southern tip of Malham Tarn; this impervious rock forms the base of the lake. Close by, where limestone overlays the Silurian, the water of springs rising in Great Close is forced back to the surface, and can be seen issuing from the ground at the southern edge of the tarn. Behind Tarn House, Fountains Fell (2,150 feet), like its neighbours Ingleborough and Penyghent, has shales and thin sandstones of the Yoredale series surmounted by a cap of millstone grit. The Malham Tarn Estate, now a National Trust Reserve managed by the Field Studies Council, was formerly the home of the Morrisons, who in the mid nineteenth century rebuilt the original Georgian mansion of the Listers; it has associations with, among other notables, Ruskin, Darwin, and Kingsley. The tarn, roughly half a mile in extent, and with a maximum depth of fourteen feet, is fringed with acid peat bog, where stages of development from open water to raised bog are demonstrated. Birds of the open water include great crested and little grebes, tufted duck, mallard, coot and moorhen. Of Malham Tarn the topographer Harrison wrote: "The Air ryseth out of a lake south of Darnbrooke, wherein as I here, is none other fish but red troute and perche." The error about the source of the Aire is understandable; he was certainly right about the fish, which are still found there.

The outflow from the tarn, known as Malham Water, goes underground at the Water Sinks to re-emerge south of the village at Airedale Springs, and a dry valley deepening to a gorge, perhaps a former course of the beck, has been cut downwards to the lip of the Cove, and to the edge of a pavement some three hundred feet above the valley floor.

On a summer's day, with car parks replete and every guest house fully booked, the streamside path from Townhead sees a procession of sightseers bound for the foot of the Cove, where the beck issues forth into the light; not till it is joined by Gordale Beck below the village does it become the Aire. House martins glide and circle about the cliff face, their purring trill amplified and echoing in the hollow; the moving pattern traced by their white rumps, seen as shining specks against the shade of ash foliage, is almost mesmeric. A kestrel screams from its nesting-ledge at higher level, apparently disdainful, like the jackdaws, of the human charade below. Naturalists may like to recall that it was on just such a summer's day three centuries ago that the "great-grandfather of English natural history", John Ray, walked up a somewhat quieter path to the foot of the Cove to record a beautiful plant "Greek Valerian, called by the vulgar Ladder to Heaven or Jacob's Ladder ... in a wood on the left hand of the water as you go to the Cove from Malham plentifully". Unbelievably, the lovely blue flower, now mostly relegated to cottage gardens in the area, still blooms here, protected by ash trees and rough terrain. In the words of the botanist Lousley: "As the eye follows the blue flowers up the scree at Malham Cove on a day when the sky is cloudless, one is tempted to follow the example of the 'vulgar' and call it 'Ladder to Heaven'."

The district is renowned for its flora, which includes mountain bedstraw and a little bloody cranesbill. Calcicoles, or lime-loving plants, abound, and it is interesting to compare these with the restricted flora south of the mid-Craven fault line, on more acid gritstone soils, where cotton grass, molinia, mat-grass, gorse, heath bedstraw and bilberry are dominant. On spoil heaps of old mines one can look for spring sandwort and the more local alpine penny cress.

There is scarcely an acre in Malhamdale where the finger of time has not traced its message; in drumlin, in uplifted scarp, in the fossiliferous reef-knolls of Wedber and Cawden. To these add the eloquent display of man's own contribution to the landscape, seen in Iron Age enclosure, stonewalling, overgrown quarry and mine working. Mineral deposits associated with the fault lines occur on Malham Moor and Pikedaw Hill, and the repaired chimney on Dean Moor is a reminder of the smelt mill, where calamine (ore of zinc) was roasted, and lead (galena) smelted with coal from the bell-pit shafts of Fountains Fell summit.

Hill fort, burial mound, lime-kiln, and drovers' track, like Mastiles Lane, a monastic road which on its way westward crosses the head of Gordale, are all patent reminders of past inhabitants of the Dales; less obvious were those remains and artifacts which have been unearthed by excavation, or brought to light from the darkness of caves.

A few miles from Malham north-westward along the mid-Craven fault line, Langcliffe Scar above Settle is a spectacular series of limestone headlands – Attermire, Settle, and Great Scar. Here at the edge of Ribblesdale in 1838 the blocked mouth of a cave was discovered. Subsequent excavation brought to light a collection of remains which was to make the find famous, and in honour of the Coronation year the cave was named 'Victoria'. The names of two local enthusiasts are linked to it; Joseph Jackson in charge of excavations, and Tot Lord who organized a collection of relics from this and other caves in Langcliffe Scar.

The discoveries in Victoria Cave were of several eras, consistent with a fluctuating climate, and a layer of clay left at the end of the Ice Age provided a useful index. Beneath this deposit were the remains of creatures typical of tropical conditions. hippopotamus, lion, elephant; above it, animal bones of a cold period – arctic fox, hare, wolf – the harpoon of a Mesolithic hunter, and some beautiful silver and bronze brooches, Roman coins, spearheads, and daggers of Iron Age refugees during the

Roman occupation. Victoria and Jubilee Caves are a pleasant afternoon's walk from Settle, by way of the 'Roman camp' and Attermire, returning via the delightful village of Langcliffe. At Winskill one comes across further evidence of glaciation in the erratics, or 'stranger rocks' left stranded on limestone pedestals; below, the gorge of Cowside Beck leads down to Catrigg Force and Stainforth.

At Winskill, the road passing northward traverses the edge of Langcliffe Scar through a miniature pass that has in its outcrops all the embellishments of the Little Big Horn. On a June day the bluffs of limestone shimmer in the heat, and it is with a feeling almost of disappointment that one sees the head of a Comanche warrior outlined against the sky turn out to be nothing more lethal than a curious Swaledale. One begins to have doubts, too, about the stagecoach that, rattling across the mesa, presently resolves itself into a renegade bulldozer extracting limestone; nor is the sweating dalesman in the driver's seat any substitute for the delectable Miss Doris Day!

The winning of limestone for sale to suburban gardeners is a thorny problem, especially in a National Park, and opinions about it may differ; but it would be a pity if views like those from Winskill were to be ruined by the scars of uncontrolled extraction.

A clear day should be chosen for the trip northward from Cowside to Halton Gill, one of the most scenic approaches to Littondale. If it is in early June, so much the better, for both spring and summer have their rewards, especially for the nature-lover, in the grey lands that lie around the base of Penyghent. Like its neighbours, Ingleborough and Fountains Fell, Penyghent is a gigantic sandwich of millstone grit, Yoredales, and limestone, resting on a bed of older slates; like its compatriot across Ribblesdale, it is impressive in its isolation. For all its mere 2,200 feet it has all the qualities one would expect of a 'mountain': unrivalled views; not one, but two, scarps, grit above limestone; and some spectacular screes and rock-falls that make the ascent at its southern end an exhilarating experience. The stretch of Pennine Way from the summit of Fountains Fell, by way of the miners' track and Dalehead, to Penyghent is a wonderfully scenic one. On any summer day, and some winter ones, walkers, tall with pack, pass by Rainscar at the foot of the two-mile trough between

the hills. On a gate by the cattle grid a new notice greets them:
"No hang-gliding ... " No doubt these perspiring travellers
will refrain from taking such liberties, though by the looks of
some of them nothing short of a jumbo-jet would get them off
the ground. But away they go up the double scarp, and one is
hard put to it to keep up with the admirable young stalwarts.
The way leads by Churn Milk Pot and across Fawcett Moor,
which with its sphagnum and cotton-grass indicates a sudden
reversion to acid conditions in the midst of limestone country.
Where pockets of glacial drift have been left this apparently
contradictory vegetational pattern often occurs. In wet weather
it can be heavy going across this section of moor; after torrent-
ial rain one may sometimes see the limestone strata on the
south side of the mountain spouting water along the bedding
planes, for all the world like a bullet-ridden water butt. In late
March when snow is melting and "the cataracts blow their
trumpets from the steep", a few days of milder weather can
bring about a transformation, especially on the limestone crags
below the summit, where mountain saxifrage (*Saxifraga oppositi-
folia*) blooms almost overnight – purple cushions hang on the
inaccessible rockface. This beautiful and specialized montane
plant, which also occurs sparingly in a similar habitat on
Ingleborough, was known to the ex-soldier botanist Thomas
Willisel, who was responsible for many early botanical observ-
ations in the area. It was he who about 1668 enabled John Ray
to record purple saxifrage "on the north side of Ingleborough
Hill, near a bog by the side of an underground river". The
habitat of the plant in the crevices and chimneys of Penyghent,
where even sheep cannot get, is an extremely dry one, and
being between a wall of cliff and a steep scree, is not the sort of
situation in which casual visitors will delight. The main
display, in April, is seen, therefore, by only the privileged.
Walkers to the summit, where on the north-west side there are
crags of gritstone, will, nevertheless, have the sight and perhaps
company of ravens, whose favourite ploy is to ride on outspread wings just off the edge of the scarp, and keep pace with
one for perhaps half a mile to the summit cairn.

In high summer, when the sacrament of the snowdrops has
been celebrated, and the annual pilgrimage to the saxifrage is
an exquisite memory, it is time for the flower-lover to visit
Penyghent Gill, which cuts a deep ravine in the limestone

before entering Littondale as Hesleden Beck. This hollow between two great hills is the epitome of all that is delightful in dales landscape – a quintessential interplay of limestone upland and austere fell – from the point where the infant beck, fresh from its birth on the heights of Penyghent, vanishes underground, to its noisy canopied approach to the Skirfare, almost three miles below.

Stand at the head of the gill in the first enclosed pasture, where it is difficult to tell wall from outcrop, or outcrop from sheep. It is an impressive setting, with Fountains Fell and Plover Hill on either hand, and Penyghent at one's back. Recline, if you will, against a green bank, and follow the sweep of the gill between sculptured slabs and terraces; note how the level line of clints cuts off the gorge at its bend; and marvel at the brilliance of limestone in sunlight. On a day of cloud, or storm, this remarkable setting can be even more impressive, and it comes as no surprise to learn that the very spot on which we have rested must have inspired primitive man with the same sentiments of awe. For this mound, green and undistinguished, the so-called 'Giant's Grave', is what remains of a late Neolithic barrow. The circular mound, about fifty feet across, has been greatly mutilated, but two groups of large limestone slabs mark the position of burial chambers.

More recognizable are the embankments and enclosures of Celtic origin found on the hillside on the south side of the gill. These derelict walls and fields usually occupy the flattened part of a terrace, often following the lines of natural outcrop. Enclosures are small and grouped together, with the remains of one or two roughly circular huts, tumbledown and roofless. Nearby on the hillside where limestone and gritstone meet, an ancient track follows the shoulder of Fountains Fell, passing along the smooth turf as a green road, still used, that connects Ribblesdale with Littondale. It is the sort of path that invites the walker, level and full of interest. Here and there a beck comes briskly down from Fountains Fell, cutting back as a waterfall into the terrace edge; but its freedom is short lived as it is swallowed by the limestone. Dry gorges are frequented in summer by ring ouzels, which nest on the rocky ledges. For a while after the birds' arrival in March one must look for these a hundred feet below in the gill, where winds are less keen; in July you will find them dispersed in unexpected places, beneath bracken, or busy among the bilberries on gritstone fells. In summer considerable numbers of golden plovers are to be found at the edge of pavements fringing Penyghent Gill where uneven stretches of grassed-over clints are favoured. It seems likely that many of these birds are either non-breeding juveniles or 'off-duty' individuals from pairs nesting on the damper peat and grassland above.

But the glory of the summer months here beneath Penyghent is the long succession of flowers, and the extended season brought about by height, exposure or abnormal habitat. Primroses and violets linger into June, and dog's mercury, wood sorrel, and anemone, normally regarded as hedgerow or woodland plants, flourish in the grikes, where there is some humus and moisture. May blossom and bird cherry herald the blooming of mountain pansy, bird's-eye primrose and bane-berry, to be succeeded by rock rose, milkwort, shining cranes-bill, and grass of Parnassus – never a day throughout the long weeks of summer when the joy of life and colour are not apparent in the haven of the gill at Hesleden.

At the end of summer as days begin to shorten perceptibly, sometimes in the evening a grey mist is drawn across the valley, veiling the solid haunches of Penyghent brooding above the gill, and the arc of enclosing hills. Fleeceless sheep, gaunt from clipping, move gently in a landscape as unreal as the sound that rises and falls somewhere at the head of the gill. It may be the cry of a belated curlew, or the wailing of a distant diesel in Ribblesdale; but those whose heart is set in the Dales will know that it is the stirring of one who sleeps in the tumulus, marking the uneasy passing of summer.

V

ROCK AND RAILWAY

FROM STAINMOOR to Ribble, over many a lonely mile, the limestone of the Askrigg block plays out its many variations – muted in Swaledale, delicate in Wensleydale, massive and dominant in Craven. Whatever form or key the limestone assumes, its recurring theme is the beauty and delicacy of its unique landscapes of pavement, pasture and outcrop. It is appropriate, therefore, that where it capitulates in the south-west to the sombre shales of Bowland it should do so with all the distinction of a great artiste at the final curtain. Here above the Ribble and Wenning the carboniferous limestone surpasses itself and has summoned up the renowned 'Three Peaks', Whernside, Ingleborough and Penyghent – a fairyland of glens and waterfalls, and a plethora of caves and potholes. In this demonstration of virtuosity earth movements have contributed their own effects in the contorted rocks of the unconformity seen at Ingleton and Helwith Bridge; manifestations of the Craven Faults, stretching away south-eastward as far as Nidder-dale, have in their turn produced some of the most dramatic scar landscape of the Dales, particularly at Attermire, Malham and Gordale. Giggleswick Scar is a classic example of a well-defined fault line; here the mid-Craven fault has resolved itself into a wall of limestone, well elevated above the millstone grit country extending southward at its feet. For half a mile or more the main Kirkby Lonsdale road skirts the base of the escarpment and motorists returning in the evening from a day out in Morecambe or the Lakes have a splendid view of the fault line as they top Buckhaw Brow, and descend towards Settle.

In the soft evening light of winter the limestone often takes on a delicate shade of pink, and its lower cover of trees a warm orange, but those who stream by towards home in the manu-facturing towns of East Lancashire and Yorkshire will have little inclination to investigate the cave at Buckhaw Top. Nor, for that matter, to take their life in their hands and stop by the roadside to see the Ebbing and Flowing Well. The days are long past when travellers in a more leisurely age were glad of the chance to rest before their laborious ascent of the brow, sitting on stone slabs to watch the rise and fall of water which, according to Camden, took place "sometimes thrice in an hour", the level subsiding "three quarters of an hour at the reflux, though thirty miles from the sea". Today the phenomenon of the underground syphon that so intrigued earlier visitors is, to put it mildly, of some reticence. But one is reminded of the story of the two locals, one from Settle, and his sceptical friend from Austwick:

"Ah doan't believe it ever does ebb'n flow."
"What for?"
"Becus ah avn't seen it, and ah'll believe nowt 'at ah
    avn't seen."
"Es ta seen thi own brains?"

Scarcely less noticeable from the main highway is the village of Giggleswick; it is all haste for a more modern version of ebb and flow, at the tea-urns, conveniences, and petrol pumps of Settle, a stone's throw away across the river. Anglian in origin, Settle and its Norse counterpart, Giggleswick, are in many ways complementary; while the former, in a manner of speaking, attends to the body, the latter, with its church and public school, caters for the mind. At Settle, the past has been pushed aside and lies in Upper Settle around the base of Castleberg, "a monstrous limestone rock that threatens destruction". Here a lime-burner was once charged with endangering the town as a result of the extraction of stones for his kiln, but the jury finally concluded that if Castleberg were to collapse, it would fall away from the houses! Today an artist's colourful impression of the rock adorns the main approaches to the town; the old road from the south over Hunter Bark slips into old Settle unnoticed, in places scarcely a grass track, and disused since 1753 when it was replaced by the Keighley-Kendal turnpike along the valley. In 1249 Settle was granted a market charter, and gradually became a centre for produce, leather, woollen goods; and cattle fairs were held three times a year. Visitors today may pause in the square and admire the balconied Shambles; conjecture on the origin of Ye Olde Naked Man Cafe beneath a more discreet effigy on the doorhead dated

1663; or be misled by the imposing façade of The Folly, an over-elaborate town house built in 1679 by one Thomas Preston who, so the story says, wished to create the impression of opulence, and in so doing beggared himself.

On Tuesdays in the square beneath the Victorian town hall a weekly market still draws crowds of locals and visitors, and traffic builds up on the A65 and shunts spasmodically through the throng. Modern shoppers and sightseers evidently find the town much more attractive than the eighteenth-century Settle which so disappointed Pennant who enlikened it to a "shabby French town", and the poet Gray, who, unimpressed, declared "there are not above a dozen good-looking houses, and the rest are old and low".

Once across Ribble Bridge the traveller who, heading west, emerges unscathed from the turmoil of tourism at Settle, may scarcely be aware of the existence of Giggleswick. A row of many-storied houses fringing a bend in the road beneath trees effectively shields the village. If Settle welcomes with open arms, Giggleswick discreetly effaces itself in a hollow and escapes the worst effects of traffic; it is, nevertheless, a shade too close to the main highway to permit of complete relaxation. Perhaps that is why its houses gather so closely around the church, as lambs seek the shelter of a parent ewe. As in so many dales villages interest centres on the church, here dedicated to St Alkelda, though seldom, one fancies, is there such a curious concentration of buildings. Venerable old houses with mullioned windows, square dripstones, and datestones of the seventeenth century are set closely around the church wall, clearly imbued over the centuries with the dignity and graciousness of its patron saint.

On an April day the setting could not be more charming as one enters the village by way of the Tems beck, a limpid stream spanned by a single gigantic slab of slate perhaps twelve feet long. Missel thrush and rook are in good voice; the fluting of the former bird fills the hollow and follows one past the tiny school. There are glimpses of woodland slopes, crocketed pinnacles, and the green dome of the chapel of Giggleswick's famous boys' school. A tractor stands in a farmyard a few paces from the churchyard, and a shaft of sunshine illuminates the datestone of a cottage – 'L.A.E. 1669'; a common dripstone encloses both window and doorhead, which bears the emblems of two spoked wheels and lozenges. Beneath the substantial lych-gate a broad flagged path approaches the church; there are more leading off into an extended graveyard, and to other gated entrances. The stone of the flags is of a beautiful blue-grey, and its smooth surface almost too refined to walk upon. This is the Silurian slate, doubtless from the quarries of Helwith Bridge where the unconformity is exploited among predominantly limestone workings; one comes across pieces of it throughout the area, as door-jambs, dairy-slabs, and gate-posts. The millstone grit of the church walls looks dark and rough by comparison, as do many of the crumbling grave-stones. The names, dates, and epitaphs on the older headstones are obliterated, but it is certain that many of the village folk below them were christened with water carried from the ebbing and flowing well in a ewer-bucket. Above the sleeping villagers, in the land of the living, the church clock sonorously marks each quarter-hour. The sound of its bell drowns for a moment the song of the missel thrush; the train leaving Settle for the long haul up Ribblesdale; the distant chain-saw; the jackdaw struggling with a twig at a hole in the masonry a few feet from the bell is apparently oblivious to all but his own immediate problem and the urgency of nest building. Not for him the marking of the hours, the sundial above the church door, the funereal yew and cypress. He lives by the sun; the primulas and daffodils below him are his clock and calendar. Daffodils by the altar, and in every cottage garden along the village street; more in the unexpectedly extensive ground behind the church. If the good folk of Giggleswick are crowded together in this life, at least they have the consolation of knowing that in the next they will have plenty of room!

In the tenth-century incursions of Norse settlers from the west resulted in the establishment of new communities, some-times in close proximity to existing Anglian villages, but more often on uncolonized higher land at the dale heads. Generally speaking, the suffixes -ley, -ham and -ton indicate settlements of Anglian origin; -thwaite, -wick, -set, and -ergh denote the Norse. There are many pleasant villages in this corner of the Dales that lie beneath the scarps of the Craven Faults, sheltered from the north and east winds that bite across the exposed pavements above them. The difference in altitude of a few hundred feet can mean the difference of a few hundred pounds to the feed bill for hungry Swaledales during a bad winter, and the folk of Clapham, Austwick, Stainforth, Langcliffe and Settle, strategically disposed against the elements, have much to be thankful for in the geological accident that produced the scarp country of Craven.

On a morning in late March I make my way along the sunken lane beneath Moughton Scar – a track along which, perhaps, many a weary packman after a hard day's bargaining at Austwick has stumbled three centuries ago to replenish his pack at Settle. Time and neglect have certainly not improved its condition. At one point the lane has become a river bed, and one can wade ankle deep, or make a strategic detour through broken limestone walls by way of the field. Near Lower Bark the last gate hung on posts of grey slate is open, and a sea of newly churned mud indicates the recent movement of sheep to the farmyard. Presently there comes a growing sound of commotion; moving dogs bark, stopping and starting as if battery-operated; sheep chorus in many keys; a shepherd yells with all the apparent hysteria of his kind. The burden of his commands is unintelligible to human ears, but the sheep understand. So do the dogs. Only the adjectives strike a chord; they are vaguely familiar, and somewhat dubious. One thing is certain – they will never be recorded with the journalistic relish of "yan, tan, tethera, pethora, pimp . . ." Actually John Hickson is the nicest fellow imaginable. His Swaledales lamb early, beginning about 5 April. After a hard winter, expect-ations are not very high, but in recent years twin lambs are increasingly common, due to improved methods of husbandry. His Swaledales appear almost diminutive by the side of his neighbour's lanky Welsh half-breds. Many of the sheep have unusual brown markings on the muzzle – a new strain, perhaps. "Oh! thi'v bin at t'treacle," John explains, in reply to my question. "It's fer twin lamb disease!" In a nearby field a drum of molasses stands upended into a trough; and the mystery is solved!

For sheer beauty of landscape, dramatic scarp, and long embracing view, this triangle of upland between the massif of Ingleborough, the Ribble, and Giggleswick, is unsurpassed, a backwater fortunately bypassed by the streams of holiday-makers heading north up Ribblesdale, or west to Kirkby Lonsdale. The artist and photographer will find subjects enough in outcrop and pavement, and along the line of headlands that culminate in Smearsett. There are woodlands of ash that frame views of Penyghent and Ingleborough as only ash trees can. Graceful of outline, late to leaf, and of softest green for most of the summer, the ash is the dominant species of this high-level woodland; perhaps its only shortcoming is its lack of autumnal colour, for ash woods invariably pass abruptly from summer to winter with none of the autumn fire of beech, sycamore and birch. In Wharfe Wood there are places devoid of grass where trees spring directly from the eroded clint, with roots as spectacular as their branches, and the steep scarp is clothed with the foliage of ashes growing on screes of an impossible angle.

It is small wonder that archaeologists, too, are drawn to the area to investigate its many caves and Iron Age sites. Roman coins and the bones of a cave-bear have been found near Buckhaw, and in the peat of Giggleswick Tarn, now drained, was discovered a Bronze Age canoe. In this area too the Brigantian chief Venutius assembled his tribes against the Romans. Defensive entrenchments were established on Ingleborough summit, and the remains of enclosures and tumble-down stone huts scattered about the ridges and pavements evidence the extent to which the area was occupied.

"What have these lonely mountains worth revealing?" asks Emily Brontë in one of her poems. Very much, it would seem, in this part of the Dales. The search for such sites is a fascinating business, but enthusiasts must be blessed with a good pair of lungs, Herculean legs, and the powers of imagination of a Picasso!

A glance at a map will reveal the Norse origins of many local place names – Austwick, Lawkland, and Wharfe. And what of Feizor – Fech's shieling – a name that owes more to the gloom of a heathen fjord than to the sunlit heights of the Yorkshire countryside?

This most delightful of hamlets would appear to have retired from the world. It nestles with its 'back to the wall' at the end of a narrow winding lane deep beneath the scars of Smearsett and Oxenber, and a gated limestone track leads over the 'nick' to Wharfe and to the quarrylands of Ribblesdale. There is a strip of green, a pump, and a shallow ford, but rarely much water to be seen. The window of a cottage set alongside the track looks out over the last gate, as if to challenge the stranger who would enter and disturb the peace. In earlier times Feizor was of greater importance, apparently, than today, for both Fountains and Sawley Abbeys held possessions here; the Hall, now a farmhouse, was once monastic property. On the summit of Oxenber with its Iron Age remains, or from the confusion of stones of uncertain origin on Pot Scar, one can look down on the roof-tops of the village, and trace the many ancient grass tracks along which passed drovers, monks and beasts when Feizor lay on the route between Fountains Abbey and its granges in Lakeland.

On these heights there is no time of the year so exhilarating as early spring, when the tiny plumes of the grass sesleria shine an exquisite blue at one's feet, and the kestrel rides on the north wind along the white walls of Smearsett. This wind that comes biting down Ribblesdale with snow flurries from a blue sky in its wake brings a clarity as no other, and reaches out into Lancashire till Pendle Hill and Bowland Knotts appear but a stone's-throw away. To the north the face of Moughton Scar frowns as if with resentment at the encroaching quarries below it, its undercut base resembling a lesser Kilnsey. On the nearer slopes a patch of almost discordant pale green marks the lichened surface of Silurian outcrop; there is more of this slate – much more – in the rock-strewn valley of Crummackdale that invites one on to the limestone heights of Sulber.

There are few landscapes more dry under these spring winds than the miles of arid clint and parched sheep's fescue that surround Ingleborough and Penyghent. It was, of course, these very conditions which prompted Iron Age man to settle here on elevated pavements and terraces, in an area predominantly cold and wet. Stumbling over the rough breast of Smearsett – an area of fragmented clint normally circumnavigated by walkers – one can make out the remains of tumbledown huts. To the south-west of the cairned summit, across the Happy Valley, a long, straight shadow marks the position of the Celtic wall, a rampart of huge blocks set on a natural rock foundation, extending for some sixty feet in a north-westerly direction. The wall, five feet high and equally wide, overlooks the remains of earthworks in the valley. Some doubts may be entertained on its effectiveness as a defensive structure, and its purpose may have been rather as a burial ground; the observer

who goes to the effort of mounting the wall at its eastern end
will observe that it points directly to Ingleborough, a fact of
some irrelevance except, perhaps, to a bibulous Brigante returning to base after a night out on the tiles (Roman)!

Pleasant in the Dales are those secluded corners which one
discovers unexpectedly. For me, there are several around Feizor
and at the foot of Ingleborough, and each comes under the
heading of a 'summer place'. At one, the clearest of becks brims
with trout and mimulus; at another, a white cottage floats
above a field of buttercups in the June sunshine. One cannot
say more without revealing secrets, and I would not rob you of
the pleasure of discovering them unexpectedly for yourself.
Suppose, however, you start at Wharfe. Not at all connected
with 'Wharfedale', but the tiny hamlet near Austwick whose
name, 'hvarf' (a nook or corner), is a fair description of its
favoured disposition. In the words of Ernest Booth, who from
Low House keeps a flock of two hundred Swaledales on the fell
where cold winds are a hazard of his job: "It's grand to git
down hoam to Wharfe; it's a different day down 'ere!" Along
the lane the manor house, formerly monastic property but only
recently re-roofed, has had the addition of a porch which bears
the mark of the Ingilby family; the datestone reads: 'W.I. E.I.
1715'. But as you leave the village on a summer's day you will
carry with you into Crummackdale a colourful sampler of
green leaves, stone cottages, and meadow cranesbill by the
wallside. For a little way along the lane the blackbird's song
will accompany you, but that of the beck will be your constant
delight until it, too, is silenced – gone to earth beneath the
white walls of Moughton. Below White Stone Wood one has a
choice of routes: to continue along the lane by Moughton Scar,
or to cross Austwick Beck and pass via Crummack Farm to
Beggar's Stile, and Sulber Nick. Among the wilderness of clint
and boulders are seen yet again the remains of Celtic enclosures
and hutments.

A Cumbrian unfamiliar with this Pennine valley, and
suddenly awakening by White Stone Wood, might be forgiven
for imagining himself back at home in Lakeland. The eye
wanders across a Wordsworthian landscape

> . . . o'er pathless rocks
> Through beds of matted fern . . .

in a setting more reminiscent of Kentmere or Longsleddale than of Yorkshire.

A clapper bridge of grey Silurian slate spans the beck, and lichened grey walls wander across grey outcropped hillsides. In places older Ordovician rock occurs as slates and shales, some of which contain the fossil remains of graptolytes and trilobites – the earth's earliest life forms. Grazing sheep, scarcely distinguishable from the rocks themselves move slowly about their 'heaf'; only when they are driven by dogs, or trail along behind a Landrover, do they become a significant part of the landscape, crowding in an unexpected spasm of activity into some nettle-grown sheep-fold normally the exclusive perquisite of wagtail and tortoiseshell butterfly. In summer, green bracken, which flourishes on siliceous soils, clothes the lower slopes, later to bring an unusual warmth of colour to the dale; indeed, it is the absence of bracken and grasses from the clints above that makes autumn the least attractive of seasons in limestone country.

When the geological era known as the Pleistocene came to an end some ten thousand years ago, accumulations of rock and debris were carried down by melting glaciers and left as 'erratics', often on high ground. Limestone upland may thus be dotted with fragments of a different rock, as at Winskill, Smearsett, and here across the valley, at Norber, where dark boulders of Silurian, visible from some distance, have been transported from the floor of the dale and stand on pedestals of limestone two feet above the surrounding surface, the older rock above the newer. The rock immediately beneath the erratic, protected by overhang from the elements, is slow to weather, the height of the platform representing the extent to which ten thousand years of erosion have affected the surrounding exposed surface. The Norber boulders may be approached from either Clapham or Austwick by way of the bridle-path of Thwaite Lane.

Many visitors come to Austwick, another village set against the side of Ingleborough. Geologists will be drawn to the low Ordovician countryside to the north-east of the village, and to the anticlines and synclines which have produced the outcrops of the Silurian, exposing unconformity where the Great Scar limestone lies along upturned edges of slate.

Limestone terrain drains quickly after rain, and streams often plunge underground, but the deposition of glacial drift gives rise to pockets of damp grassland with a flora approximating to that of millstone grit moorland. An example of this can be seen on the northern side of Oxenber, on the lower slopes of which flourishes a community of calcifuges that includes sphagnum, sundew, cotton grass, cross-leaved heath, and bog asphodel. Heather, heath bedstraw, and silver hair-grass are found on drier slopes. By contrast, the barer limestone summit of the hill boasts a lengthy list of calcicoles, including various cranesbills, thyme, and rock-rose. Naturalists will also find interesting the mossland of Helwith Bridge, Austwick, and Lawkland, whose variety of specialized vegetation may be determined by the nature of its water supply. Cotton grass, heather, bilberry, cowberry, cranberry and bog cinquefoil are found within the zone of raised peat, and at its margins, fen woodland includes alder, birch, willow and bog myrtle. The drying out of the surface as a result of improved drainage has promoted the growth of birch scrub.

Austwick, the 'eastern settlement', is a study in grey and green; a village once noted for its market before it was superseded by neighbouring Clapham; a market cross with a new shaft proclaims its former importance. On the dated doorhead of some of its larger houses the letter 'I' commemorated the Ingilby family, who in 1573 purchased the Hall, a fortified manor house.

Perhaps the chief claim to fame or notoriety are the people of the village themselves, known to posterity (and without offence) as the 'carles of Austwick'. An enterprising lot, by all accounts. They worked the town fields near the village, shot rabbits, gathered sticks and limestone on Oxenber, were troubled with trespassers, and according to legend, were naïve enough to indulge in some far less likely activities. On one occasion, it is said, they lost the only knife in the village by leaving it in some outlandish place, having marked the spot – by a cloud shadow! They learned, too, that the most expeditious way of removing a grass-grown thatched roof is not to have a cow eat it off.

Having noticed that good weather occurs in the season of the cuckoo, the villagers determined to ensure a plentiful supply of sunshine by keeping the bird permanently. To accomplish this they built a wall around the tree where it was perched. History does not record the sequel, but it is interesting to note that the prosaic Whitaker declared with unwonted lyricism that the village was "warmed by the reflection of the sunbeams". Perhaps the carles of Austwick were less simple than legend has painted them.

From Crummackdale one can return by field path and grass track over Swarth Moor to Settle, from which road and railway lead directly into Ribblesdale; or, more importantly for the economy of the dale, they lead *out* of it, bearing the slate and limestone for which the locality is famous. The railway is, of course, with us throughout the dale on the rising gradient – the 'long struggle' – from Settle; we shall meet it again at Ribblehead, Dent, and Garsdale, a thread along which is strung some of England's finest landscape.

The entrance to Ribblesdale is not always prepossessing. A broad road enters a broad dale, set on the grand scale of Penyghent and Ingleborough. Ancient pack-horse and drovers' tracks filter in as one progresses up-dale. Yet it is of the details that one becomes aware; the distraction of weir, paper mill, and quarry working. At Stainforth Foss, where a lovely pack-horse bridge spans the Ribble, and salmon still leap below the waterfall, a caravan site occupies the river bank for most of the summer, and is all too obvious from most of the heights between Settle and Penyghent.

Stackhouse and Langcliffe face each other across the river; the latter, a quiet backwater surrounding a village green, was once the property of Sawley Abbey. A shop, a fountain and a well-placed seat offer welcome distraction before the steep climb to Victoria Cave and Attermire. The northern end of Langcliffe Scar is a prominent feature, dropping down by Winskill to Stainforth, a village divided by the river. Here pack-horse tracks once crossed the Ribble, and the hamlet was a halting place for travellers and beasts on their way between York and Lancaster. Friar Stainforth, successful under Sawley Abbey, and now flourishing as a centre for caravanners, lies on the eastern bank; on the west side Little (or Knight) Stainforth failed to prosper. Its most striking building is the old hall, a three-storeyed yeoman's house built in the second half of the seventeenth century by Quaker Samuel Watson. Along this section of the valley one can also look out on the west bank for the conical-shaped eminence of Smearsett, and for the green terraces of Anglian strip cultivation above the larger village.

From Stainforth, the journey up-dale, once a harrowing experience along a narrow and tortuous road, has been considerably improved, and one now has an even chance of evading the procession of stone-laden juggernauts that are gradually removing Ingleborough from quarries at Horton and Helwith Bridge. Here limestone and slate are quarried on a large scale, the latter as a legacy of the fault line which has exposed the blue-grey Silurian at Dry Rigg. In the worked-out quarry above the workers' cottages at Foredale a classic exposure has left the horizontal beds of limestone supported on a mass of uptilted slate.

Horton-in-Ribblesdale, mentioned in the Domesday Survey as 'Hortune' (the farmstead on muddy land, or river flats), straggles along the road as if in indecision, concentrated near Douk Gill Beck, close to the church. Three stoops and a flagged pathway of slate lead up to the Norman doorway of St Oswald's; the font and nave are of the same period and are impressive in their lack of adornment. High in the western window a small fragment of coloured glass, thought to show the mitred head of Thomas à Becket, may be part of a larger work and have come from Jervaulx Abbey. Half a mile along the sharply angled road, a second concentration of cottages, houses and bungalows by Brants Gill Beck and the Ribble has tourist amenities; camping, caravanning, fishing, potholing and walking are catered for. Horton, not the most elegant village in the Dales, is a base for underground expeditions to, among others, Alum Pot, Long Churn, Hull Pot and Gingle Pot. From Penyghent descend walkers on the Pennine Way, perhaps to refresh themselves, for an overnight stay, or to sign the record book at the Penyghent Cafe before proceeding north to Hawes.

In 1876, after a gargantuan task which had lasted seven years, the Settle–Carlisle railway brought the line to Horton, and quarrying was developed. Today, the industry flourishes, quarries are extending, and limestone is despatched continuously by road and rail to all parts of the north of England and to Scotland.

The landscape now is dominated by the long form of Penyghent – a lion couchant, with a pronounced double scarp at the head, or southern, end. Apparently vertical screes give little idea of the paths that traverse them, especially those at the foot of the lower cliff of limestone, which is well known to botanists. At Horton church the hill pleasantly crowns the roofs of cottages to complete a study in grey; from the approach to Ribble Bridge it sits squarely above The Crown along the road updale; it is reduced to aesthetically pleasing proportions above the velvet green of the rounded drumlins which crowd the valley floor. Cattle stand silhouetted on them, and dry-stone walls outline their contours as if with a pencil line, accentuating the 'basket of eggs' form of the drumlin field. The road twists and turns towards Selside and dives beneath the railway, whose embankments, unkempt in September, are best remembered for their continuous carpet of primroses in spring. Selside – the 'shieling by the willows' – originally Norse, is mentioned in the Domesday survey, and until the Dissolution was the property of Furness Abbey; in fact, most of the dale was once shared by Furness, Fountains, Jervaulx, and Sawley. It is difficult to imagine the hamlet, formerly an isolated settlement, as having a fair; and an inn; and unlikely as it may seem, the barn-like building, still with the remains of a chimney stack, and overhung by an ash tree, was once the town hall. As the modern road winds round it one can hardly fail to notice the name plate it bears – SELSIDE, in large letters that once adorned the local signal-box.

Following the tarmac road up-dale one tends to take for granted the present-day lines of communication, which appear so firmly impressed on the landscape. One may be unaware of the presence of earlier routes established before transportation depended upon the wheel – the network of roads seen today as bridlepaths, overgrown lanes, or green tracks. Their courses are marked in the valleys by pack-horse bridge and ford, and on the hills by ancient 'crosses' or markers. Upper Ribblesdale has many such forgotten ways. They run down the dale below Penyghent, from Littondale, and Greenfield, and through the wild country at the head of Langstrothdale. A road over Cam Fell, known to the Romans, came over to Gearstones from Bainbridge. You see it from Selside as a white track disappearing over the hills to the north-east. Across the Ribble, Newhouses and Birkwith mark a traditional route from Ribblehead; there are pack-horse bridges at Ling Gill (now a nature reserve) and Thorns Gill near Gearstones; and it is possible that a Roman road from Long Preston once passed that way to Dent.

One such track leaves the main road above Selside, and between limestone walls passes below the ridge of Simon Fell (2,088 feet) over Sulber and Long Scar, to Austwick and Clapham. In summer one joins the company of walkers, and potholers in wet suits, and at North Cote farm, suitably refreshed and having paid a small entrance charge, ascends a private but well-worn track towards a clump of trees on the hillside. Here within a walled enclosure the beck disappears into the overgrown abyss of Alum Pot. Notices warn visitors of the dangers, for the pothole has had its casualties. A few hundred yards away at the far corner of the field, the cave and passage known as Long Churn gives a second access to Alum Pot for those suitably equipped, terminating in a gallery within the main shaft.

The northern end of the Ingleborough massif ends in Park Fell, on whose flanks, at over 1,100 feet, and following a natural terrace on the hillside, is the mile-long strip of woodland at Colt Park, now a nature reserve administered by the Nature Conservancy Council, from whom a visiting permit must be obtained. This area of about sixteen acres, described by botanist J. E. Lousley as "one of the most remarkable and uncanny in Britain", is an example of aboriginal woodland, predominantly ash, on limestone pavement. In June and July it contains an unexpected variety of uncommon plants, in a habitat which at first glance may appear unfavourable. Angular Solomon's seal, baneberry, wood cranesbill, giant bellflower, variegated pansy, herb paris and lily-of-the-valley occur there, the latter two very sparingly. Sheep are excluded by the nature of the terrain, an examination of which can only be accomplished by a hazardous scramble over limestone clints, and among grikes of unusual depth, dangerously overgrown. Visitors must be active, and proceed with care, but in June the rewards are great. Having spent a rapturous hour among the trees, one can sit at the edge of the wood on a boulder, shaded by the fresh green of ash, rowan and willow. Pausing to admire the view of Penyghent and Ribblesdale, the naturalist will be quietly aware of activity close at hand. A stoat, hunting in the interminable crevices, raises his head repeatedly from a clump of belated dog's mercury. The sibilant note, like a sharp intake of breath through pursed lips, insistent from overhanging boughs, shows where the spotted flycatcher is building against a buttress of limestone. Wheatears sing, a sharp spasm of sound, as they mount in aerial song flight from a nearby walltop. The call of a ring ouzel marks the position, no doubt, of a distant pothole, where young are being fed, and a pair of oyster-catchers pipe their way over the wood, heading riverwards. The willow warbler is the commonest bird of Colt Park; in June, there is scarcely a moment when his silvery cadence, near or far, is not heard.

As the weeks go by, you may return and taste the exquisite wild strawberries; or later observe the orange fire that consumes the leaves of the cranesbill; then bid your fond farewells to the restless echelon of Ribble oystercatchers, daily more anxious to answer the call that takes them round Ingleborough to Morecambe Bay. In February your pilgrimage may end at the railway cottages by the bridge, with Gauber High Pasture ice-bound and impassable. Or you may battle your way down to the river, by way of Lodge Hall, formerly Ingman Lodge, and find snow packed against the iron-studded door, with its flanking halberds, and datestone 'C W 1687'. There you may encounter Mrs Mason busy with a shovel, or Mr Mason, muffled up within a Landrover, jockeying up to the main road with hay for his sheep. Weather is a constant theme in these parts, and this strangely quiescent three-storeyed house from another century has seen its fair share of winters.

Our journey up-dale is almost at an end. The Cam and Gayle Becks have joined forces, and are augmented by countless rills that emerge from the underground caverns of Runscar and Thorns. Ribble has been born and is on its way to Blackpool, where its dubious origins are long forgotten, and any speculation as to its birth is purely academic.

In the elevated hollow of Ribblehead, a grand junction of daleheads and river systems, The Station Inn and a mobile snack-bar preside over a triangle of green seldom free from activity, from which walkers and cavers mount their weekend and holiday safaris. Tents, caravans, or mountain rescue are seldom absent. A prolix signpost flings out its arms horizontally, though it is safe to say that those adventurers who operate from Base Camp Ribblehead seldom work in that plane. Those with packs ascend to the heights of Ingleborough, Whernside, or Cam Fell. The rest, usually in the regalia of the pot-holer, descend – to the underground world of Holme Hill, Capnut, Cuddy Gill, Batty Wife and other caves.

Perhaps the most remarkable feature of this austere gathering place is the twenty-four-arched viaduct, 165 feet high, which spans the hollow of Batty Moss, carrying the old Midland Line to the foot of Whernside, and into Blea Moor tunnel. Here during the years of construction a shanty town on Batty Green was the home of some two thousand workers engaged in building the viaduct and nearby tunnel. A post office, library, school and hospital were incorporated in the village. Many men perished, as a result of conditions, accidents, and a smallpox epidemic. The churchyard at Chapel le Dale was enlarged in the early 1870s for the burial of over a hundred navvies who succumbed during their stay at Batty Green.

A short distance along the Ingleton to Hawes road, formerly a Roman road and a section of the Richmond turnpike, is Gearstones, now a house, but once an inn. Here at the end of a long drovers' route south via Mallerstang and round Widdale Fell Scottish longhorns were gathered for sale, twice a year, and one tries to visualize the scene two centuries ago – the many hundreds of cattle crowded into a vast enclosure; dogs and lads; the inn crowded with English buyers and Scottish sellers, agreeing each evening in 'mutual drunkenness'; drovers sleeping rough in their plaids bivouacked behind a wall, and the smell of burning peat. Two miles away across the brown waste of moorland, and beyond the track to Dent, Newby Head, then also an inn, was the headquarters of butchers.

Today visitors may pause at Gearstones to explore the delightful Thorns Gill, on the modern Craven Way. Its gorges and pools are crossed by a footbridge near Far Gearstones, and by an ancient pack-horse bridge, now almost obscured by ash saplings, half a mile downstream. There are caves for the exploring, and limestone boulders on pedestals. In summer it is the flowers that will claim attention – rock rose, milkwort, and bird's-eye primrose; in September, when rowan berries hang scarlet against the white textured rock, blackbirds erupt from the depths as one approaches. Then the air is filled with thistledown, and parties of twite and goldfinches frequent the streamside. Thorns Gill is very much a place for the nature-lover and artist, who will presently find a wilder beauty along the immaculate ribbon of tarmac that climbs to Newby Head.

This last section to the head of the pass carries a flavour of the Scottish highlands, and the view south is superb, especially during winter, when the setting sun brings a glow to Gayle Beck, and Ingleborough, from this angle many hills in one, is stark against the evening sky.

At over 1,400 feet the road eases over into Widdale. Redshaw Moss, a waste of peat hags and rising grassland, is passed on the right. Sheep are strung out along the roadside, and for the motorist the way can be hazardous, especially at lambing time. As one glides down-dale, Widdale Fell grows in stature; its highest point, Great Knoutberry Hill (2,203 feet), unseen from the east, is most easily climbed from the coal road above Dent Station. Views from the fell, especially westward, are very good; to the north beyond its two tarns it falls in a long ridge to Sandy Hill, above Appersett.

Descending to Hawes by the main road, one passes between the new forestry plantations of Widdale Foot and Snaizeholme, the latter at the entrance to a side valley. Here one may look out for the short-eared owl, which hunts in daylight, quartering the rough hillsides at tree-top height, and usually showing little fear of man. Such plantations are often the haunt of the black grouse, a large ground bird which sits closely, but which is capable of strong flight. In these young forests of Widdale, and over the fell in the more extensive ones at Greenfield, both species breed; the nest, sometimes at the foot of a spruce, is difficult to find, but foresters come across them in the course of their work. One of the most amusing sights in winter, when the birds may wander in search of food, is that of the large ungainly form of the grouse installed in the topmost sprays of a bare birch tree, to which the bird has resorted for catkins.

The prospect of welcoming new species which a changing ecosystem brings is an exciting one, but is tempered with the realization that the scenic impact of the regimented conifers will not be fully appreciated for perhaps twenty years. It is to be hoped that, unlike the Enclosure Acts two centuries ago, these new forests will not herald the start of yet another era in the changing face of the Dales.

Nearby, on one occasion, I spoke to Jack Metcalfe, whose family has farmed in these parts for centuries, and who told me of some projected alterations planned for his farmhouse. Protracted negotiations with the local council had so far produced no results – except resentment on the part of the Metcalfes. "Ye can't do as ye like wi yer own stuff these days," he complained. As I passed down-dale two forestry workers were busy with wire and mallet, erecting a new section of fencing on the hillside. Above the infant pines of Snaizeholme a patch of sunlight drifted upwards over Stags Fell and lit the distant road to Buttertubs. There are some curious anomalies in the National Park.

VI

CLIMBERS AND CAVERS

THE LONG CATERPILLAR of children edges forward in the darkness. Above spluttering candles, projecting a grotesque interplay of shadows that dance on damp walls, the amplified drip of water penetrates a chorus of subdued voices, and cool air fans the cheeks. Above the murmur, a Yorkshire voice asserts itself and the hissing carbide lamp, stationary for a moment, silhouettes the cloth-capped figure of the guide.

"The rock underneath is Pre-Cambrian. It is seven hundred million years old. Above is limestone; this is only three hundred million years old . . ."

The measured emphasis and well-timed pause elicits a chorus of "Oh's" from suitably impressed youngsters, and one cannot help but have the greatest regard for a man who, after experiencing some difficulty in counting nine (old) pence from thirty children, can pronounce with equanimity "only three hundred million years old".

The caterpillar crawls forward. It stops before a calcite formation – the 'Organ-pipes'. Our guide warms again to his subject. There is an exclamation of wonderment. The children lean forward to hear the music. Mouths open. Candle boards droop. There is a smell of burning hair . . .

At the end of the cave an illuminated grotto looks down at its own image in a clear pool. A final burst of rhetoric from the old man; this final exposition brings down the curtain in an awed silence.

It is a long time since the late Arnold Brown, some-time guide of Ingleborough Cavern, charmed the children in the days when it was an adventure by candlelight to sample the subterranean delights of Clapdale. But time moves on, and 'progress' has come to this corner of the Dales, as it has to many others. Today electric light illuminates the cave, an immaculate highway bypasses the village, the estate woodland has become a nature-trail, and the manor house is an information centre, where every aspect of study and leisure are catered for. It is a familiar story, repeated at Malham, and Grassington, and Aysgarth; yet as coaches follow each other into vast car-parks, one begins to wonder if, perhaps, too much has been done. The excursion is now an incursion; certainly the discovery of some parts of the National Park is far less of an adventure than it used to be. In fact, one is sometimes left with the feeling that there is little left to 'discover'; that it is a case of saturation rather than stimulation, and that revelation has begot exploitation. To all this there is no ready answer; in the meantime, the cohorts of students on environmental studies storm the bastions (or what is left of them!) of Malham, and the blanched face of Gordale becomes a monument to the passing of yet another era of dales history.

Ruminating thus as I came along Thwaite Lane from Austwick to Clapham on an April day, I had to admit to myself that, despite the mental stimulation of walking, no solution to the problems of conservation had presented themselves by the time I had sighted the village. At eight hundred feet and beyond the watershed of Buckhaw the changing topography to the south is most evident. The westward drainage gathers the waters of Austwick and Clapham Becks to become the Wenning, further augmented by Keasdon Beck which carries most of the run-off from Bowland. The rise southwards of the upland of this ancient forest is so gradual as to give little idea of height, though much of the land reaches about 1,500 feet. Prominent along the flattened lines of gritstone fells that stretch coastwards are the rugged protuberances of the Knotts – outcrops of millstone grit that form a spectacular barrier between Lancashire and Yorkshire. The aspect from the north of these fells, usually seen against the light, is sombre except in winter, when dark crag and heather are relieved by the russet of bracken slopes.

There is a growing impression of woodland as one approaches Clapham; stands of trees alternate with green fields and grassed-over lynchets, below which the road takes a sudden turn to the 'New Inn' into the village. Clapham, which boasts a cave rescue post, an information room, and the headquarters of the Dalesman Publishing Company, is divided down the middle by a beck spanned by a multiplicity of bridges – five, we are told – and ends at the parish church of St James. Like Arncliffe church, it is a place of snowdrops at the end of winter, but perhaps the finest sight of the year is to be had in March, when the gates of Ingleborough Hall open on to an unbelievable display of aconites, a fitting introduction to grounds that once belonged to the botanist, collector, and explorer Reginald Farrer, the 'Father of English rock garden-ing', whose collection included plants from all over the world. A nature trail named after Farrer now passes through the grounds of the Hall, which lies at the top of the village. The doors of grey and cream cottages open on to the road itself, or on to narrow strips of garden, colourful in April with daffodils and blood-red tulips. Round the corner one passes into the estate grounds by a sawmill (once a bobbin mill), and follows the trail by an artificial lake along Clapham Beck. This section of the walk is through woodland, and a great variety of trees includes holm oak, Spanish chestnut, Corsican pine and bamboo. Beyond the wood a valley beneath scarps with formations of tufa – sponge-like deposits of calcium carbonate on moss – leads on to Ingleborough Cave.

Of the delights of the cavern some mention has already been made. Today the many visitors who follow the wooded nature trail, or who come by the fell path and Clapdale Farm, can journey a third of a mile beneath Ingleborough, exploring its many formations – the Elephant's Head, Pillar Hall, and the Abyss – by electric light, though perhaps less romantically than the Victorian ladies who once arrived in waggonettes and who, looping up their skirts, made the tour of these underground wonders by candlelight.

The cave was first explored in 1837, a few years after the construction of the artificial lake above the village. James and Matthew Farrer and their helpers breached a natural barrier of stalagmite at the back of an existing cave to release a small lake of water and bring to light a new system of passages. These penetrated Ingleborough to the extent of half a mile, and were to become a part of the present show cave which ends at the Pool of Reflections; passages beyond are reserved for enthusiasts.

> Ingleborough, Whernside and Penyghent
> Are the highest hills 'twixt Tweed and Trent.

While not quite correct in its superlative, the doggerel does serve to underline the fact that the Three Peaks of Craven have at least something in common. Along with Gragareth they manifest the same geological structure, with summits of millstone grit above carboniferous limestone, and ancient Pre-Cambrian rocks below; a giant sandwich of permeable limestone some 600 feet thick between impervious grits and shales. Water flowing down the upper section thus disappears into the middle layer, usually at an altitude of eleven or twelve hundred feet, and gradually dissolving the limestone, passes along the fissures and cracks, enlarging joints and bedding planes on its way to the impervious slate below, where it emerges as springs, or from the mouth of a cavern. In this way cave systems are excavated along the horizontal bedding-planes, and vertical joints may be enlarged into the shafts we call pot-holes. It follows therefore that the majority of pot-holes and caves of engulfment (those with a descending entrance), for example Diccan Cave in Ribblesdale, will be found at the upper level of the limestone layer; caves of debouchure (in which the floor has an upward trend) will be at a lower level, as at Great Douk.

A cave located in a scarp may, due to a collapse of its roof, become a gorge or rift in the hillside, as at the nearby Trow Gill, an impressive tree-surmounted corridor where the path from Clapham mounts the hillside. Sometimes a roof collapse or subsidence below ground gives rise to grassed-over symmetrical hollows, or 'shakeholes'; small holes with drainage, or damp depressions, are known as 'sink-holes'.

On the hillside above Trow Gill, one can look on a summer's day from the deep shadow of the ravine across to the shining pavements of Long Scar. A litter of boulders among the grass below the scarp may well be the debris of a collapsed roof. There is every reason to suppose that the deep gorge, now dry, was once a water course, perhaps a meltwater channel or a surface gutter of Fell Beck which now plunges into that most famous of pot-holes, Gaping Gill. The Gill was discovered by a Frenchman, M. Martel, who in 1895, assisted by his wife, descended in twenty-three minutes with the help of a rope-ladder, a life-line, and a portable telephone; it was here that dales pot-holing was born. Visitors can on occasions in summer-time make the descent by block and tackle under the supervision of caving organizations. Three hundred and forty feet below in the darkness of the main chamber the stream passes underground, and joining with the water from Ingleborough Cave, reappears at Beck Head – a course verified in 1900 by the addition of coloured chemicals by the Yorkshire Geological Society. The hypothesis is that the cave system is in some way linked with Gaping Gill, but it remains for some intrepid pot-holer to establish the connection.

One thing is certain – that there is still much to be discovered in the limestone hills of Craven.

Close to the crossing of the River Greta by the A65 a signpost in large letters announces "Ingleton – Beauty Spot of the North". It is a pity, one feels, that this should appear so close to a transport cafe, a scrapyard, a welter of petrol pumps, and a warehouse. Still in high hopes one detours by a bevy of boarding-houses with unrivalled views of a railway viaduct, passes a yard of caravans, and so into the village. It may now begin to strike even the optimistic that Ingleton is singularly unimpressive, and has few pretensions to the aesthetic. It is a Beauty Spot without Beauty, has a Coal Mine without Coal, a Granite Works without Granite, and a church so disenchanted with the place that it continually tries to remove itself.

Basically the historical background of Ingleton is not unlike that of any other dales village; Thomas Gray, in 1769, declared it "a pretty village . . . at the foot of that huge monster of nature – Ingleborough". Today its beauty is obscured beneath unlovely development and all the amenities occasioned by modern tourism. It has a manor house, and a church whose nave has been rebuilt more than once, due to subsidence. The village had an annual fair where leather and produce were sold, but later the emphasis was on cattle. In 1849 the railway arrived from Settle, and a few years later was extended to Sedbergh. The valleys of the Doe and Twiss (which unite to become the Greta) with their glens and waterfalls, whose potential had so far not been realized, were cleared of growth and obstruction by an active 'Improvement Association'; paths and handrails were provided, and the trains brought in a stream of visitors. At Whitsuntide in 1887, a bumper year, it was reported that "nearly every cottage was open for the sale of hot water"; in 1893 an estimated 100,000 visitors came to see the 'wonders of nature', in particular, the four and a quarter miles of 'Falls Walk'.

Ingleton has had other industries – quarrying, wool and cotton; the remains of a mill, with upper storey doorways boarded up, and strangely quiet, stands idly by Thornton bridge. Coal has been mined for hundreds of years on the east side of the village, where in the mid nineteenth century buyers with their horses and carts would gather overnight for the next morning's load. After many vicissitudes the mine was reopened in 1913, and the miners accommodated in a concentration of red-brick houses which became known as the 'New Estate'; twenty-four years later production ceased due to lack of funds.

But the village has at least one redeeming feature. Away from the main street, with its crowds, commerce, and commotion, one can, perhaps after a hard day's walking, take refreshments in a little green oasis by the Twiss. Here in April there are daffodils where the mill race once ran, and the cawing of rooks and song of the dipper sound a pleasant accompaniment to the unflagging voice of the beck, where once, it is said, rival landowners vied with each other for the patronage of early tourists bound for the falls.

However dubious may be the attributes of Ingleton itself, there is no gainsaying the attractions of its environs, centring on Ingleborough (2,373 feet), the first great bulwark of the Pennines in the west. Like its near neighbours Whernside (2,419 feet) and Penyghent (2,273 feet), it is subject to all the vagaries of weather occasioned by its proximity to the Irish Sea. Here on its flattened summit the Brigantian leader Venutius assembled the northern tribes against the Roman invader. Although much of the defensive stonework now lies scattered around the summit, aerial photographs show quite clearly the remains of circular huts and an entrenchment running over half a mile along the edge of the scarp. The height and qualities of Ingleborough have always been beyond question. In the mid sixteenth century, botanist Thomas Penny, hunting for cloud-berries on the hill, referred to it as "Mount Ingleborrow, the highest in all England"; Housman gives the height as 3,987 feet – seven hundred feet higher, in fact, than Skiddaw in Lakeland. This illusion of height is understandable, as it is in the case of any mountain seen in its entirety from base to summit. Suilven, for example, in Sutherland, has this same impressive appearance, though its height is little different from that of the Yorkshire peaks.

To approach Ingleborough from Bowland Knotts or from the Lune valley, turning into Chapel le Dale, is to see the mountain at its most impressive; small wonder that John Ruskin expressed "the vague sense of wonder" with which he "watched Ingleborough stand without rocking". Climbers, pot-holers, and geologists find much of interest in the area, and in early April botanists climb to the limestone crags to see the mountain saxifrage. It is as well to remember, however, that hills of this height should be treated with respect, especially in winter, when mist is frequent, or under snow; the same blizzard that leaves sheep buried behind a dry-stone wall can render a limestone pavement lethal. There is a story of one wanderer who unwittingly strode across a cornice in Gaping Gill, and of the remains of other unfortunates whose relics were found long afterwards in cave and pot-hole. The mind goes back in winter to the scanty peat or wattle huts of the Brigantes; hard pressed as the defenders were, they could scarcely have occupied the summit throughout the year. There are many routes up the mountain, perhaps the finest being the one from Clapham via Trow Gill, which presents the right element of surprise on arrival at the summit, from which the views into Lancashire, Yorkshire and Cumbria are superb; to watch the sun set over Morecambe Bay from the triangulation point in spring or autumn is an unforgettable experience. Other routes include the ones from Newby Cote, Crina Bottom, and The Hill Inn.

Below the summit cone an extensive pavement flanks the western face; White Scars and Raven Scar border Chapel le Dale with its many pot-holes and caves - Great Douk, Bruntscar, Meregill Hole and White Scar. The latter, a popular show cave, is a master cave, which collects over a score of drainage channels from the mountain above. Entrance was achieved by way of a pool at the point of debouchure, now drained. It was first investigated in 1923 by Christopher Long, who negotiated a low passage about 75 yards long. Half crawling through water in a tunnel at times only two feet high, and with a candle on his head, Long forced his way through obstacles to reach the first waterfall - now the Water Chamber, with its beautifully tinted stalagmites. These are formed by the deposition of calcium carbonate held in solution, an incredibly slow process, and colours are caused by the presence of salts of iron, copper or lead in ground through which the water has passed. Enlargement of the entrance and further modifications, supervised by the late Tom Greenwood, have made it possible for visitors to walk comfortably along half a mile of the main system, viewing the many formations – Buddha, The Angel, Pulpit Rock, and so on. Tom's daughter Mabel, some-time manager of the cave, will be remembered with affection for her kindnesses to thousands of visitors, and, not the least, for her delectable home-made scones served to so many ravenous schoolchildren at the entrance to the cave. Weathercote Cave lies close to the tiny church of St Leonard, from which the dale takes its name. The origins of the church are obscure. Once a chapel of ease to the parish of Bentham, it was partly rebuilt in 1869, but a record of its dedication dated 1554 reads: "Rychard Gybson of Yngleton, to be buried in the churche of Saynt Leonard . . . ny unto the place wher I have kneled . . ." Weathercote Cave, a hole in the rocks 100 feet deep, has long been a showpiece. From behind a large rock known as Mahomet's Coffin, wedged between the vertical walls, a waterfall pours down into the depths. One can descend by means of steps and, looking up into the sunshine on a summer morning, may be granted the sight of a rainbow, "for colour, size, situation, perhaps nowhere else to be equalled". This scene impressed J. M. W. Turner who included Chapel le Dale in his annual painting tours. For a drawing of Weathercote Cave he was paid the sum of ten pounds. Turner painted widely in the Dales, and according to Ruskin, their influence lingered; many a picture done later in his Italian journeyings "were recorded by him with a love, and delicate care, that were the shadows of old thoughts and long-lost delights, whose charm yet hung like morning mist above the chanting waves of Wharfe or Greta". Beyond The Hill Inn, which lies on the route of the Three Peaks Walk, a widening view at the dale head, dominated by Whernside, extends to Blea Moor. One can follow the road to Ribblehead and Hawes passing the viaduct of the Settle-Carlisle railway; walkers may take a track to the right by Scar Close, noting the strip of high-level ash woodland on the clints of High Glauber Pasture, and rounding Park Fell, will presently arrive at Colt Park in Ribblesdale.

The *pièce de résistance* of Ingleton is undoubtedly its falls and glens; they are at once a geological text-book and a unique scenic experience. The rivers Doe and Twiss, from Kingsdale and Chapel le Dale respectively, cut their way down-dale in a series of wooded gorges to reveal a geological strata which includes hard grits, conglomerates, slate and mudstone; the latter, beautifully marked with felspar, is quarried near Beezley Falls, where the Twiss thunders through a wild ravine amidst a confusion of rocks and trees. The Craven Fault Line has also added to this classic demonstration. Its dislocation is evident in the tilted limestone at the entrance to Swilla Glen; at Pecca, slates and grits are noticeable in outcrop and pathway. The beautifully scenic walk upstream along the Doe culminates in the rocky amphitheatre of Thornton Force, where water falls over forty feet from a sill of limestone lying on the upturned edges of Pre-Cambrian slate.

The falls walk is usually done in clockwise fashion, the connecting leg being a green lane which passes the farms of Twistleton Hall and Beezley's. Here, on a summer day, you may come upon a party of schoolchildren with rucksacks, enjoying a well-earned rest and a cool drink by the farmyard. A gaudy cockerel and his concubines claim attention, perhaps, or there is a drying of feet after an over-exuberant crossing of the stepping stones by White Scar Cave; one girl has a pre-packed box of mineral stones (a memento of her visit to the cave), and another, a compass (already broken) from a souvenir shop in the village. A late-comer arrives in the lane, clutching a blood-stained handkerchief to his knee.

"Sir, that new lad's cut 'is leg." (A single voice.)

One pretends not to have heard.

"Sir, that new lad's cut 'is leg." (Chorus.)

One wonders why 'new lads' never have a name. I examine the cut – a red gash beneath a dirty rag. I apply a glass of milk and cream soda to the patient, and ask how it happened.

"Ah fell on a gr . . ." (Hesitation.)

"On a what, Albert?" I ask.

"On a gr –, er . . . er . . ."

"Gryke?"

"Yes, that's it!"

"Does it hurt, lad?"

"Naw, it's jus' that ah can't remember t' name!"

Three cheers for 'Environmental Studies'.

After the scenic orgy of the Doe, one begins the descent by

the Twiss, a series of dramatic glens and falls – Beezley; Rival; Baxengill, below a bridge viewpoint; Yew Tree; and finally, Snow; not forgetting Cat-leap, in the tributary of Skirwith Beck. The round trip takes about two and a half hours; but with children or photographers allow much more. The latter should be rationed to one film per mile. Most visitors come in summer, but the best time is in spring or autumn, after overnight rain. A winter day after frost can add a new dimension to the glens of Ingleton.

VII

WHERNSIDE AND WATERFALLS

TO THE NATURALIST, the hills and dales of the Pennines are a treasure house, with a wealth of plant and animal life sometimes regulated by human activities, and sometimes unique in areas less affected by the hand of man. In a variety of terrains, landform, vegetation, and wild life are determined basically by the underlying rock structure and by the formation and characteristics of its soils; peat moor and grassland on millstone grit, limestone pavement, and cultivated valley are all distinctive habitats. Much of the interest for the ordinary visitor will centre on the commoner birds and flowers; and in one sense, it is a pity that rarer species like the lady's-slipper orchid always seem to get publicity. To the experienced naturalist the specialized and less common plants and creatures are a source of delight. Mountain saxifrage. bird's-eye primrose, globe-flower, mountain avens, and the various orchids, have always been held in high regard by the botanist while the ornithologist will be gratified, perhaps, by the sight of short-eared owl, peregrine, or harrier. As a naturalist one has certain ambitions – the discovery of a species new to the area, or the once-in-a-lifetime encounter with a rarity; into this category comes the dotterel, a small and remarkably tame brown wader which in its migration northward in spring passes along the Pennine ridges. It has a predilection for the higher summits where it sometimes lingers for a few days, usually in small parties, or 'trips'. From time to time its passage has been observed in May; there are records from Pendle Hill, Ingleborough (misguided bird!), Whernside, High Seat and Wild Boar Fells.

Those who have the audacity to seek the dotterel on the high fells must have a good deal of optimism as well as enthusiasm, for the odds against the intentional sighting of an extremely small creature on an extremely large mountain are infinite. However, on a cool and blustery May morning I struck across the fell from the head of Kingsdale, along the boggy flank of Whernside, a quieter, less frequented mountain

than Penyghent and Ingleborough – though the stony plateau
of the latter would appear ideally suited to the needs of the
bird. Visits to Baugh and Great Shunner Fells had yielded
nothing; at least Whernside would have superiority in height.
So I argued as I struck across the boggy western flanks of the
hill and pushed hard against the wind to make the last few
hundred feet to the summit on that wild spring morning.

The approach from the west is always most rewarding, if
only for the sudden impact as one steps over the final ruinous
dry-stone wall on Cable Rake and finds the mountain no
longer there! Below, the impressive viaduct of Batty Moss
crosses the valley, and above it, on a platform of hags, the edge
of exposed peat traces an intricacy of dark lines, circling and
meandering with a certain symmetry.

Seen almost vertically downwards from this height, it
appears an abstract pattern branded on the level surface as if
with a hot iron; indeed, in May the hue of the fells is still
sombre, with browns predominating. Vast areas of rushes add a
touch of colour to the hillsides; at first glance these beds appear
to grow in a haphazard fashion on the slopes, but on closer
scrutiny are seen to follow a definite progression, marking the
lines of drainage. Here and there the brilliant emerald of moss
covers the surface of wet flushes, relieving the general brownness. Five hundred feet below the summit, on Greensett Moss, a
border of the same green fringing the edge of a tarn is freckled
with white dots; there are more on a tiny island, where the
speckles are whiter and the effect more concentrated. Occasionally one can detect a movement of the pattern, which, viewed
through a telescope, resolves itself into a small colony of nesting
gulls, virtually immobilized by the gusting wind. Its blow sends
a darker shadow racing across the steel-grey waters, dashing
the sitting birds with spray; at almost three thousand feet on
the hilltop there are few signs of life. The weather-bound
wheatear which one disturbs is snatched from the summit wall
and hurled down the scree-scarp; his white rump flashes
momentarily, like a piece of paper blown from the fingers. At
this height the landscape, bereft of foreground, has lost much of
its brownness; the grey wind has drawn a veil over the
neighbouring hills which stretch away ridge after ridge, in all
directions. Its nearer neighbours, Gragareth and the isolated
mass of Ingleborough, are silhouettes of mauve, and north-

ward, beyond the pale ghosts of Baugh Fell, Blea Moor, and Great Shunner Fell, the ridges melt into Cumbria and the northern dales.

On this day in May, under a west wind, the landscape, vast and melancholy, is without substance beneath or heaven above, a corridor of summits. On one of them at this moment the dotterel may be riding out the windstorm on its way northwards. But not, it would appear, on Whernside; the dotterel hunter must have not only the lungs of a superman, but an unbounded capacity for persistence. Although senior partner, as it were, of the renowned triumvirate of Yorkshire peaks, Whernside has more affinity with its near neighbour Gragareth (2,250 feet) than with the isolated masses of Ingleborough and Penyghent. Its name is a corruption of 'Quernside' (Cweornside) – a hill providing rock for millstones. The latter peaks stand conspicuously on their pedestal of limestone, dignified and aloof, and distinguished of profile; on Whernside the limestone is less evident and dramatic, its outlines less distinctive. It lies hunched at the head of Ribblesdale, reaching out towards Gragareth, with which it forms the southern wall of Dentdale.

There are many recognized routes to the summit of Whernside. On the long haul from the south-west by Scales Moor one is accompanied by a drystone wall of phenomenal length, first of limestone, then of gritstone in its later stages. This walk of fourteen miles is for a long summer day, but there are other shorter, if steeper, routes, from Chapel le Dale, by Bruntscar, or by Winterscales and Force Gill with its spectacular crag and waterfall. The upper part of the mountain forms a long whaleback, with a group of tarns at the northern end of a ridge frequented during the breeding season by black-headed gull, golden plover, and dunlin, which feed at the water's edge and nest in a well-hidden hollow, usually on damp moorland. In the 1930s the triangulation pillar on Cable Rake was the subject of a dispute by objectors who favoured the original and considerably less formal cairn of stones. The incident itself may be of little importance but it is good to know that, unlikely as it may seem in such a little frequented spot, there are people who cherish, and are ready to come to the defence of, the remote corners of the countryside.

From the lower slopes of Whernside the view, limited by

the spurs of Ingleborough to the east and Leck Fell to the west, is nevertheless an extensive one down dale towards the Lune valley. Beyond the A65 streams meander through rolling green drumlin country; and clear of the fells the rivers Greta and Wenning pursue their parallel course westward to be joined by drainage from the Bowland moorland. The Roeburn and Hindburn, wild and delightful, flow down by Goodber and Tatham Fells to join the Wenning, uniting at Wray. Like many other hill villages at the foot of steeply scarped gritstone upland, Wray has been subject to flooding when rivers rise quickly after heavy rain. Exceptional conditions in 1967 brought widespread devastation throughout the area, and reached disaster proportions at this village; new building by the bridge testifies to the severity of the incident.

Virtually within sight of the county town of Lancaster on the banks of the Wenning, the adjoining Yorkshire townships of High and Low Bentham are fourteenth-century market centres with Victorian overtones. Some of the older houses bear eighteenth-century datestones, but church, town hall and grammar school, once the rectory, are products of the nineteenth century. A hundred years ago flax spinning and bleaching was carried on; river, mill and sandstone cottage follow the familiar pattern of Pennine textile villages below gritstone upland. There are currently attempts to project a new image of 'Bentham in Wenningdale', with one eye on the Yorkshire tourist; the other has always looked towards Lancashire's 'brass'!

The main road enters from Lancaster, but there are other spectacular approaches, like the one from Slaidburn via Cross o' Greet, which climbs over the ridges of Bowland through fells sufficiently wild and remote to accommodate one of the largest breeding colonies of gulls in Britain; where peat is still cut; and to which the hen harrier has recently been attracted as a breeder.

The green mound of Castle Hill by the Greta dominates the approach from the west to Burton in Lonsdale, as celebrated now for its trout fishing as it was as 'Black Burton' in the eighteenth century for its potteries. Coal was obtained locally. Silk and wool weaving flourished at the beginning of the last century, but pottery ceased in the 1930s.

There are many pleasant hamlets that lie hereabouts in the

vales of Lune, Greta, and Wenning, but few visitors stop to
admire them. Cars and coaches of children and sightseers pass
swiftly through, drawn irresistibly, and perhaps understand-
ably, to the much chronicled high lands of Craven, particularly
Ingleton. A few turn aside, and passing by Thornton-in-
Lonsdale, perhaps note the church of St Oswald, with its
Norman tower; round the corner the remains of the ancient
stocks stand by the road that leads to Viking's dale.

Kingsdale is an example of a Pennine valley in its simplest
terms – a straight, glaciated valley with an entrance blocked by
moraine. In its secluded and uncomplicated length of five miles
it is cradled between the mass of Whernside and Gragareth; a
diminishing trough enclosed by the magnificent limestone scars
of Keld Head and Braida Garth. There are few dales without a
hamlet of some sort, but one farmstead at Braida Garth, and a
second at Kingsdale Head, are the. only habitations in this
valley. It does, however, have its fair share of visitors, most of
whom belong to that select company of 'night-workers'
known as cavers and pot-holers. I have never been able to
determine conclusively the difference between the two, except,
perhaps, that the former operate in a horizontal plane, and the
latter, with the additional equipment of rope and ladder,
engage in the vertical. On one occasion I did come across a
helmeted caver in a wet suit emerging from a cave near Horton
in Ribblesdale, who, in reply to my query, declared of his
pot-holing colleagues, "Oh! they're the ones who have
accidents!" *Facilis descensus averno!*

Whatever the distinction – if any – the enthusiast of the
underground will find much with which to occupy himself in
and around this splendid valley; at weekends and holidays
there are considerably more folk *below* the dale than there are
on its surface. On a Sunday evening the road is edged with
vehicles; ladders, boots, sweaters, and ropes are much in
evidence, and the smell of bacon and beans pervades the
twilight of a cave in the hillside where a fire has been lit. Here
after a day spent 'grafting' underground tired pot-holers meet
in a *camaraderie* known only to those who have the distinction
of seeing the nether world of Kingsdale by the light of a
National Coal Board lamp.

Few districts of Craven have such a remarkable concentration of underground systems. Along the valley side, a

'master cave' runs for about eight hundred feet, with water at each end, and above Keld Head Scar along the line of the Turbary Road – an ancient grass track used by peat cutters – there is a long succession of caves and pots. The old track follows a natural terrace above the scars, and it is along this line that water from Gragareth enters the limestone, percolating through the many cave systems to make its exit several hundred feet below at Keld Head. Most of these 'pots' have been known at least two centuries; as one caver informed me: "To find new caves you have to dig or dive for 'em!" One system follows another for a mile or so along the 1,300-foot contour line – Kail, Swinsto, Simpson's, Rowten, and Jingling Pots – a whole selection of gashes in the limestone, from the innocuous to the downright dangerous; the slopes of Gragareth are not to be recommended under misty conditions. At the northern end of the track, below the Turbary Pasture, a tree-surmounted scar looks down on the valley road. Here a trickle of water disappears among the rocks of a ravine, and in a comparatively treeless valley, this coppice on the hillside offers welcome shade and a fine viewpoint on a sunny summer afternoon. The white bed of Kingsdale Beck draws a straight line down dale to Braida Garth; at Keld Head its waters reappear, augmented with those from Rowten Pot. Subsequently it is known as Thornton Beck, and then, the Doe.

Sitting beneath a pine at this vantage point, one gets the initial impression of a dearth of life on these bare and arid heights – an impression which is presently modified as eye and ear become attuned to the midsummer day. A pair of oyster-catchers in black and white livery pipe across the dry shingle of the beck a hundred feet below, busy with their young. A dark circling speck in the blue above Braida Garth resolves itself into a soaring buzzard which is presently lost against the darker background of the hillside; this large predator, largely a feeder on carrion, is not an infrequent sight in these western dales. Closer at hand, the sun is caught in the wings of a brood of flycatchers as they move across the shadows where the branches of an ash tree overhang the gorge. Back and forth a thousand times along the same aerial paths, throughout the long July day; for almost three months this sheltered hollow will be their world. So too with the grey wagtail whose 'weet' of expostulation echoes in the ravine, where a late brood has just fledged.

A sudden commotion beyond the drystone wall and the flailing of branches mark the presence of a small herd of black bullocks, which have moved into the shadow of a beech tree and are tearing at the lower branches.

Set beneath an archway of stones, and approached by steps, a dark opening framed with cranesbill and spleenwort leads into an unexpectedly lofty chamber – the Great Hall of Yordas Cave. Two hundred years ago the adventurous cleric John Hutton, having procured "a guide, candles, lanthorn, and tinder box" at the Church Stile (now The Marton Arms) at Thornton, made Yordas his first cave of north Craven, no doubt enjoying the contents of his basket of refreshments at the entrance afterwards. His *A Tour of the Caves* contains an account of the visit. In the inner entrance a number of pendulous rocks and a sloping floor of mud are negotiated to give access to a stony stream, normally shallow, which constitutes the floor of the main chamber; after heavy rain this is rendered temporarily inaccessible. Formations include the Map of Wales, the Bishop's Throne and the Chapter House, a 'windowed' chamber at the foot of a waterfall. The name 'Yordas' commemorates, it is said, a mythical Norse god or giant. A good torch and stout boots are necessary for the occasion; the provision basket with which the enterprising Reverend John equipped himself is an 'optional extra'!

North of Kingsdale Head Farm a gated tarmac road winds and dips up the final mile to the head of the valley, and over White Shaw Moss (1,553 feet). Just short of the summit of the pass a brown waste of bog and rushes inclines steeply up the flank of Whernside, and one cannot help but marvel at the skill and labour of the drystone wallers who pursued their craft literally to the summit cairn; on one slope above the moss the angle is so steep as to require the use of hands in climbing. After a century and a half the wall stands firm, along with the stone 'men' that mark the path over the edge, where the angle of incline alters – a reassuring sight indeed, one fancies, to many a shepherd caught out in the mist.

I can think of no view that stirs the imagination like the one that presents itself at the point where, having passed the rough lane to derelict quarry workings, the road begins to dip towards Dent. In a matter of seconds Kingsdale is dismissed, as quickly as one might turn the page of a book; overleaf, a new dale, new horizons, a new decor – a green hammock slung between ridges in a breathtaking panorama of all that is best in Pennine landscape. The contrast between Kingsdale and Deepdale is most marked, not only in the latter's breadth and luxuriance, but in its impression of enclosure. It is, in fact, a side dale of Dent, but the transverse wall of Rise Hill effectively effaces its entry, and appears to seal off Deepdale at its lower end. A long wall on the lower slope of Whernside passed along the valley side, sometimes rising, sometimes falling, but roughly coinciding with the 1,000 foot contour line, the upper limits of the green intake; on the nearer slope the division is less noticeable, especially where lines of trees follow the course of innumerable streams that rush down to join the main Deepdale Beck. Typical of these is Gastack Beck, which gathers the many drainage channels from Green Hill and Great Coum, before passing over a limestone sill in a delightful ravine. Those who have passed this way in summer will have paused by this clearest of pools, deceptively deep and overhung by trees. Gastack Force hides its beauty in deep shadow, and the colours of the rock face in the dripping crevice behind the waterfall, where it is possible for the active to scramble, are overlooked. A stone's-throw up the hillside, beyond a copse of ash trees beloved of redstart and tree pipit, a small, more intimate grotto is reserved for primrose and wood sorrel, which bloom exclusively for the benefit of the dipper whose abode is by the waterfall. In these glens the ash is the dominant tree, but a fair admixture of rowan, birch and sycamore ensures a colourful reminder of the changing season in autumn. The narrow tree-lined lane, with its enthralling glimpses of meadow and farmhouse at Platt, Hollinbush and Scow, as one passes downdale, will be remembered for its flowery banks; herb Robert, shining cranesbill, and tall elusively-mauve bellflower are a delight in July, when Rise Hill hangs like a pale backcloth in the summer heat, and the road to Dent is a dream.

Cotton grass on millstone grit

Fossil crinoids, Ribblesdale

Mountain avens, a dales rarity

Globe flowers, Garsdale

Golden plover, Oxnop Scar

Oystercatcher, Mallerstang

Woodcock

Bird of the conifers—goldcrest

Kingfisher in flight

Sandpiper, Lune valley

Fox on screes, Feizor

Dalesmen in Widdale

Jack Metcalfe sounds the forest horn, Bainbridge

Mallerstang; the road to Appleby Horse Fair

Two dales market towns. *Above* Hawes; *Below* Kirkby Lonsdale

VIII

THE IDYLLIC DALE

LIKE PLAYERS on a stage the Dales have their exits and their entrances; not to observe them in their proper season and direction is to do less than justice to their setting. Dentdale is a good example. For a dale so intimate there are a surprising number of approaches, by road, of which the least attractive is the main one from Sedbergh. It is often said that the Scottish raiders sweeping south across the estuaries of Morecambe Bay, or inland towards the plain of York, overlooked the devious road to Dent, tucked away across the Rawthey behind the hilly bastions that block its entrance. To leave the valley by this route is a different matter; with all the delights of the dale behind one, the sudden and expanding view of the Howgills comes as an unexpected climax.

The descent from Barbondale, too, gives alluring glimpses of these same shapely hills, that rise into view above the shoulder of Combe Scar, a dark amphitheatre of shattered slate produced in part by glacial action. As at Cautley, one may here look out for peregrine and raven, corpses of the latter bird once fetching 2*d*. each from the churchwarden of Dent.

The descent to Gawthrop on a day in mid October is particularly gratifying; rowan and briar bright with scarlet berries, the warm glow of bracken on hillsides, and fine autumnal sycamore aflame about the farm and cottages of the hamlet. The same colourful effects can be observed if one approaches by way of Deepdale, with the added brilliance of birch trees; here in July, the road from Gastack is adorned with the pale but elegant blossoms of the great bellflower. To arrive in Dent (the name implies the dale, not the town) in summer is soon to become aware of its affinities with the west. Hedge-rows with high banks, and a fair mixture of may, briar, hazel, and holly are common on lower ground; there is a marked absence of lynchets in a landscape that is pastoral, though corn was formerly grown and the dale had its mills, as at Gawthrop and Rash. With its higher rainfall the valley is greener than

97

many of those to the east. There can be few places more luxuriantly green than the ten narrow miles of this 'terrestrial paradise', enhanced by the brooding austerity of Rise Hill, Whernside, Great Coum and Crag Hill.

It has an intimacy that becomes apparent when, after traversing the miles of moorland from Gearstones and Newby Head, the road loops down beneath the arches of Dent Head Viaduct. At this point trains on the Settle to Carlisle railway, fresh from their dark passage 500 feet below ground level in Blea Moor tunnel, continue their aerial journey along the flanks of Widdale Fell, climbing steadily to Aisgill summit; Dent Station, two and a half miles down-dale, is itself 1,145 feet above sea level, on what must be the most scenic route in England. Those who, a hundred years ago, doubted the compatibility of a railway and a rural setting, need not have worried, for this one, far from being incongruous, has become a part of its surroundings. While its economic impact on the dale was tremendous, its visual one has, discounting its viaducts, been minimal. The line swings towards Dent Station in a grand curve, on a ledge high above the valley, the track concealed, for the most part, in a cutting, and often fringed with snow fencing. The sudden appearance of a train, visible for no more than a few seconds, and rolling by at twice the height of Blackpool Tower, never fails to amaze. Yet despite the enclosed nature of the dale, with its steep hillsides, regularly spaced becks and walls, and general impression of isolation, this unlikely and unobtrusive railway brings a sense of unity to these lovely uplands. On a stormy evening when cloud comes heavily down on Wild Boar and Baugh Fell, the fleeting glimmer of light from the carriages of the Clyde express can be a source of great comfort.

At Dent Head a green oasis of sycamore, bird-cherry and firs fringe the turbulent gill; there are more spreading a green canopy beneath the viaduct, covering the scar of an old quarry. Here among a June abundance of wood cranesbill one can still pick up fragments of dark limestone, the so-called 'Dent marble'. A number of beds of this and grey limestone are exposed in the gills of Dent and Garsdale, and the exploitation of this rock became a flourishing industry during the first half of the nineteenth century.

Below the viaduct the road levels out, closely accompanying

the infant Dee which flows in a shallow bed of limestone over a series of steps and beneath many small bridges that lead to scattered whitewashed farmhouses; at Deeside one gives access to a splendidly placed youth hostel, formerly a shooting lodge. These isolated smallholdings are a feature of Dent, a legacy of Norse settlement in a dale which escaped colonization by Angle, Dane, and Norman; 'Dent Town' is its only village, and this lost its long period of dominance early in the nineteenth century after the construction of the turnpike road through Sedbergh. A pastoral economy begets a certain independence in the outlook of its people, a forthright race of yeoman stock whose circumstances have been well chronicled by Mary and William Howitt, Adam Sedgwick, and by Robert Southey, who, in The Doctor, coined the phrase "the terrible knitters e' Dent" ('terrible' meaning, of course, 'hard working'). As might be expected, Quakerism found a ready audience in these dalesfolk, and a Meeting House was set up at Lea Yeat.

On winter evenings it was once the custom to have social gatherings in each others' houses, where dalesfolk would meet to knit, and, perhaps, to listen to stories around the hearth. Adam Sedgwick describes the scene:

> there was a blazing fire in a recess of the wall; which in early times was composed of peat and great logs of wood. From one side of the fireplace ran a bench, with a strong and sometimes ornamentally carved back, called a 'lang settle'. On the other side of the fireplace was the Patriarch's wooden and well carved arm-chair; and near the chair the sconce adorned with crockery.

A mile from Dent Head at Arten Gill a second viaduct spans a gorge in the hillside where in the last century black and grey marbles were levered out of the hillside and sawn at High Mill, remarkable for a waterwheel sixty feet in diameter. At Low Mill the stone was polished, and from the little works at Stone House a variety of articles including tombstones and chimney pieces of 'Black' and 'Fossil' were sent by road, sea, and canal to London, Newcastle, Carlisle, and Preston. One can picture the loaded carts making their way up-dale, and the extra horses needed for the difficult scramble from Dent Head over to Ribblesdale; or the long journey down Dentdale, and the rattle of carts through the narrow street at Dent Town, and so to the turnpike at Sedbergh. After the arrival of the railways stone was sent by rail, but shortage of labour and competition from imported Italian marble put an end to production by 1900. At the foot of Arten Gill a cluster of buildings almost hidden among trees is all that remains of the marble works, and, in the words of Dr Raistrick, "their harshness has been ameliorated". George Raw, white-washing and 'odd-jobbing' before shearing begins at his farm at Cow Dub by The Sportsman Inn, was less euphemistic about the disappearing past. "Thi' keep tekin' stones away, like; ther's nowt much left!"

There is an air of seclusion, almost dereliction, about this overgrown corner at Stone House, tucked away behind broad canopied sycamores and copper beeches. Mossy walls, resplendent with the colourful foliage of shining cranesbill, do their best to usher one past the large house, perhaps once the home of the mill owner, with its tall chimneys, outdoor stair and eccentricity of windows – eight in all, and no two alike. In the gill bottom, a litter of boulders, the remains of a wall or two, and a clump of rowans carry the eye upwards to the graceful arches of Arten Gill viaduct. Unbelievably, a station for Dent was almost built at this point – and indeed, at Blea Moor, seven miles from the town! The walled track, steeply inclined beneath the viaduct, climbs towards Widdale, with a branch that passes below Great Knoutberry Hill on its way to Garsdale.

Some distance above Lea Yeat a twisting road climbs to the outpost of Empire of Dent Station, which is, according to Baddeley, "the hardest in the kingdom for anyone to hurry to walk up to . . . The road is generally considered two miles up and one down". Here, five miles from Dent Town at 1,145 feet, the highest English main-line station was built, and once had rest rooms, canteen and loop sidings, a refuge against atrocious conditions in winter when blizzards are a hazard. A shanty town close by housed almost four hundred railway workers, and at the height of activity, when Rise Hill tunnel was under construction, the hamlet at Lea Yeat had workshops and a brewery; two miles up-dale a licensed house known as the 'Wonder Inn' also catered for construction workers. In an atmosphere of the Wild West, well-paid navvies ate, drank, and fought with bare fists, tending to disappear during bad winters, and at haymaking time. The tunnel at Rise Hill, or 'Black Moss', driven through limestone for three-quarters of a mile, proved unusually difficult and had to be reinforced with iron.

Now the waiting-rooms on Dent Station are locked and wired up; one is an outdoor centre run by Burnley schools. On the platform, time literally stands still – at 5.20, to be precise, but whether a.m. or p.m. it is impossible to tell. Nor, for that matter, will anyone know the day, month or year when the station clock finally gave up the ghost. For many a long year, it seems, it has stared white-faced from Platform One at trains that no longer deign to stop to exchange the time of day. The station sign, on the other hand, is a new one, and bears the ram's head emblem of the Yorkshire Dales National Park, whose authority operates an occasional seasonal service, known as 'Dalesrail', to this and several other remote stations. Otherwise you must come to the spot by road, savouring the view and the quietness, or in summer to watch the nesting martins who have taken possession of the waiting-room. And where else in Britain can you stand on a railway platform and watch a ring ouzel feeding its fledglings, as I did one day in June?

The road that climbs to Dent Station and continues to Garsdale is both a scenic and a historic route. Known as the 'Galloway Gate' or 'Coal Road', this former drove and pack-horse track was a branch of the ancient cattle route from Scotland via Mallerstang. Along its upper levels by Mossdale Moor a number of green mounds were once the Garsdale Colliery. Coal from the main limestone was used domestically in the Dent, Garsdale and Sedbergh areas during the eighteenth and nineteenth centuries, being transported along the 'coal road' first by pack-horse, and then, in the last century, by simple carts, rough and noisy. Usually no buildings were needed, but pits were connected by tracks, now grassed over. Some coal was used for lime burning, and field kilns were normally built close to the pits, and often below them, so that transportation of fuel was facilitated. There are scores of such kilns still to be seen – for example, by the Dee at Stone House, and a cunningly contrived one built into the walls on the east side of Galloway Gate, close to the green mounds of the pit. A load of lime coal cost about 7d., fine coal 11d., and smithy coal, a shilling. With the coming of the railways local pits were discontinued, as was the use of field kilns when large quarries were opened and lime burning became a technical operation.

Much of the reduced limestone was used for the improvement of marginal land during the eighteenth century, when

cattle droving was at its height. It has been suggested that up to
100,000 beasts were moved annually from Scotland by traditional routes along the Pennines. One such drove road came
south from Carlisle by way of Mallerstang, branching to
Gearstones at the head of Ribblesdale, and to Malham, where
cattle fairs were held. At the latter fair, on Great Close, as
many as 5,000 head of Scottish beasts were sometimes gathered,
to be fattened for markets in the south, or sold to butchers. The
nineteenth century, with its enclosing and improvement of
land, and the transportation of cattle by rail to new centres,
brought an end to the era of the 'kilted cowboy'.

Those who travel on a good day by the ancient 'Coal Road',
now metalled, between Dent and Garsdale, will find the route
an equally splendid one in either direction. A foretaste of its
delights can be had by Dent Station. In July after haymaking,
when the chequerboard of fields varies between pale yellow-
ochre and rich green, the vision of the dale seen over banks of
meadowsweet and cranesbill is exquisite. There is a neatness
and regularity in its rectangles of colour that is repeated in the
darker hues and regular lines of walls and becks on the steep
southern slope of Rise Hill. Higher, beyond the conifers of the
new plantations at Dodderham Moss, the narrow strip of
tarmac winds between generous green banks and drystone
walls, with here and there a small sheep fold. One summer day
I found a carpet of fleeces laid out on the grass, and draped
across the walls. A shepherd had just finished shearing, and as I
watched, he penned the last ewe, and began deftly to roll and
tie the fleeces, throwing them into the back of a Landrover.

In one's enthusiasm for the widening view it is easy to forget
the hardship that went into the building of these walls almost
two centuries ago, when wallers walked miles, often in darkness, with their 'baggin' of bacon, cheese and oatcakes, to earn
half a crown (12½p) a day.

At almost 1,800 feet at the edge of Mossdale Moor with dark
peat hags above and the delicate grey and green of limestone
below, the Coal Road begins its descent into Garsdale, unfold-
ing a panorama that literally compels one to stop. If Dentdale
captivates by its intimacy and detail, this view northward does
so by its breathtaking distances. It is most impressive in winter,
with snow on the tops giving majesty to some of the highest
ground in the Yorkshire Dales. Below, a grey continuous pall

of mist follows the course of the valleys. It is too cold to pause
for more than a moment, but time enough to note the nature
of the extended plateau, with its high points isolated as white
protuberances; from the north-west – Rise Hill (1,825 feet),
Baugh Fell (2,216 feet), Swarth Fell (2,235 feet), Wild Boar
Fell (2,324 feet), High Seat (2,257 feet), Great Shunner Fell
(2,340 feet), and Lovely Seat (2,213 feet). Of these, the
distinctive outline of Wild Boar Fell is a conspicuous centrepiece. In summer, a more leisurely survey can be enjoyed.
Reclining against the grassy bank of an old pit, one can pick
out details in the green landscape immediately below – new
forestry on the slopes of Baugh Fell; the high valley of Grizedale, slung like a hammock between East Baugh and Swarth
Fells, its entrance blocked by moraine, now dark with heather;
and the slopes of Abbotside Common, at the head of the Ure.
At the northern end of Galloway Gate those who wish to leave
Dentdale have a choice of three routes: Garsdale and Sedbergh,
and the Howgills; Mallerstang, Kirkby Stephen, and the Eden
Valley; or Wensleydale. If you decide on one of these prema-
turely it would be a pity, for then you will have missed the
'town' of Dent, and no one should do that.

It is no exaggeration to say that, from a traveller's point of
view, the white walls and narrow cobbled streets of Dent rank
in reputation with Aysgarth, Hardraw, Gordale Scar and
Bolton Priory; what the Bridge House is to Ambleside in
Lakeland, so is the main street of Dent to the Yorkshire Dales.
To call it Olde Worlde would be to do it less than justice, for
the village, despite its thousands of visitors, is anything but a
fossilized façade for the benefit of the tourist. Yet it is certainly
old world, despite the changes which have brought the
caravan, the curio shop, and the car park to its environs. In the
middle of the last century Dent's most famous son, Adam
Sedgwick, regretted the loss of "picturesque old galleries, which
once gave character to the streets; and in some parts of them
almost shut out the sight of the sky"; mercifully the cobbles
and the solid white-walled houses remain, and there are now
one or two shops. Formerly, there was only one, and if it was
impossible to fulfil your requirements there, you did without.
'Ya'll 'av to do as thi' do i' Dent" was a familiar saying in
surrounding districts for 'going without'.

After the influx of Norse settlers, in the tenth century and later, the village, British in origin, became a lordship under Arkel and Aykfrith. Eventually it was forfeited to the Crown, and under the direction of twenty-four sidesmen, in 1670 the land was transferred to freeholds.

The pioneer geologist Adam Sedgwick (1785-1873), son of the local vicar and Woodwardian Professor of Geology at Cambridge, whose granite memorial, known locally as 'the chipping', stands at the centre of the village, is commemorated on a tablet in the church as a man who "loved to dwell on the eternal power and godhead of the Creator, as revealed in nature". He wrote eloquently on past life in the dale, and his accounts, often idyllic, are much concerned with dalesfolk; for example, the knitters of stockings, jackets, mittens and caps for the woollen industry centred in Kendal. Men, women and children knitted, some with a needle fitted into a sheath on their belt; and hosiers ran small mills at Stone House and Rash. At the beginning of the nineteenth century there were fairs, sports and a market, and butter was sold in an out-building of The George and Dragon. Coopers made butter barrels and there were several blacksmiths. Wig-makers and tailors flourished, and Dent, larger then than Sedbergh, was the polling and postal centre. In 1834 a Methodist chapel was built on the site of a Friends Meeting House, but by the middle of the century the picture was changing to one of increasing poverty and depopulation. The grammar school, built in the corner of the churchyard and endowed in 1603, was closed in 1897. Some relief for the poor of Dentdale came in the second half of the century with the late enclosing of land and, between 1869 and 1876, with railway construction; both of these activities, however, brought an element of unrest and friction to the valley.

The view from Lea Yeat is that of a green and lengthening dale, and one imagines its impact on astonished passengers between tunnels on the railway five hundred feet above. The scattered nature of the farmsteads becomes increasingly apparent. They stand out clearly, white-faced against green hillslopes, connected to the roads by narrow ascending tracks, often walled or hedged. With their neat porches, little crofts, and fruit trees, these simple houses are a delight to the eye; the sound of their names is just as pleasing – Dillicar, Blands, Rowantree, Birchen Tree, and Clint. At Cowgill, down a walled lane set in buttercups and hedge parsley, a row of three cottages by the river is known as 'Weaving Terrace', once 'Weaving Shop'. In the past it has served as mill and brewery, but is now occupied by older dalesfolk. By the chapel of St John, a tablet set in the bridge is inscribed "The bridge reper-ed at the charg of the West Riding A.D. 1702". In those days the workmanship was infinitely more dependable than the spelling. The churchyard is another essay in floral appeal; blues of hyacinth, speedwell, and bugle; white of may, parsley, and horse chestnut blossom. Mildewed gravestones mark the over-grown graves of whole families of dalesfolk bearing names that have written the story of Dent from the first yeoman farmers who built the solid homesteads around us and moulded the landscape of the dale – the Capsticks, Sedgwicks, and multi-farious Middletons and Masons. As one old dalesman informed me: "Wi're all connected i' Dent!" Len Sedgwick, who lives close by, was told by a curious visitor, "You must be connected to Adam Sedgwick." "Aye," replied Len drily, "or 'e were connected to us!" Strangers are not easily received. As one local told me: "Owd Joss came 'ere when 'e were three, and died when 'e were ninety-three, but 'e were still an off-comer!" I asked one Dent matriarch, sitting outside her cottage at Weaving Terrace, how long she had lived in the dale. "Oh, a few years," she replied.

Standing back from the road at Gibb Hall, the setting of Mary Howitt's 'Hope on; hope ever', a cottage and the ruins of a large mansion stand side by side; a smaller building close by that now houses a Volkswagen was once a smithy. Little seems to be known of the origin of the ruin, which may well be built on the site of an earlier house. Its porch and lintel have almost disappeared, and stonecrop decorates its front, which has double round-headed windows under a common dripstone. Ducking beneath a low lintel, one steps into the house part deep in nettles. Fragments of splintered beams a foot square lie across the main room, minus its upper floors, and open to the sky. A massive chimney breast with a salt cupboard, and a rear well where presumably a staircase gave access to the bedrooms, complete the scene of dereliction, and further investigation would be unwise. Only the swallows and the butterflies may come and go with impunity in this crumbling shell of a fine house, where one can only speculate on those who once lived there. A barn close by showing signs of recent repair bears a datestone 'I.S. * 1680'. It seems possible that the road has been re-routed at this point; certainly the arrangement of the houses at Gibb Hall is a curious one, seen in a modern context. It is surprising that this mansion has been allowed to decay in this way; but even more surprising that it has not been sold for renovation. But as dalesman John Allen so succinctly put it, "Thi' don't sell land i' these parts, thi' buy it!" All the same, several overtures have been made about its purchase. Recently, a car drew up at Gibb Hall house, next door, and the driver made an offer for one window of the ruin.

The Dee, with all the waywardness that characterizes rivers flowing over limestone, plays its seasonal game of hide and seek along this part of the valley. There are waterfalls and rapids; at some points fords cross its shallow bed. At others, the river in spate has cut deeply into angular layers of limestone, forming dark pools beneath the overhang of rock. Here, at two points called 'Tommy' and 'Nellie' respectively, the gorges are spanned by a footbridge, and well-marked paths through meadowland lead to farms on the south side of the river. Impressive as these gorges are, they are only curtain raisers to what is to follow at a spot near Gibb Hall.

They call it 'Hell's Cauldron'; a misnomer – until you have seen it in action. It has many moods. Under normal conditions, it is an impressive place; after rain, disturbing. At times of spate, it can be fearsome. The gorge of the cauldron is an epitome of all that delights and impresses in the wooded limestone land-scape of the dales, and being in Dent, finds its perfection in its scale. It is difficult to know what to compare it with. For weight of water, perhaps Aysgarth. In impact, a lesser Gordale Scar. Easegill Kirk will also come to mind; or Trow Gill, enclosed, and with water. Water, at times with all the might of Whernside and Widdale behind it, pouring from a stepped aperture in the rocks. In summer, when ramsons still flowers in the hanging woodland at its entrance, and ivy and honeysuckle bines suspend themselves above crystal pools, it is a delight to venture down on to the dry watercourse, shut off by high scarps, and canopied with branches. A little way upstream a rocky amphitheatre with deep undercutting bars further progress. Viewing this idyllic dale from some vantage point, it is hard to imagine the forces that are periodically involved in the green and hidden tunnel of Hell's Cauldron.

Similarly concealed are Dent's secret byways – the network of back-roads and narrow rutted lanes set deep under hedgerows of hazel and hawthorn. These run down to the river, and, as the dale nears its end, a little way up the hillside. Approached by the main road, Dent Town appears before one set on an eminence; perhaps that is why the sudden view of it below one, from an unusual angle close to Low and High Halls, comes as a surprise. Of the two, the latter is perhaps the more interesting building, typically plain but solid, with mullioned windows, and two cylindrical chimneys topped by a ring of pebbles. A datestone set in the wall reads: 'per T W I 1625 re edificat per T A D 1665'. Another grey old house, also at the end of a rough road, is Bickerside, with a projecting porch and three round chimneys. Below Gawthrop a group of cottages by a green mark the site of a former corn mill, and above it Combe Scar traces the line of the Dent fault. Salmon running up the Dee as far as Barth Bridge nearby were once taken on sharpened sticks. On the final reaches of the river the dale's affinities with Lakeland are plainly manifested; in the Silurian slates that outcrop in the river bed, and in the round chimneys of Bickerside. Nor must one omit mention of a third reminder, in the more appetizing form of Kendal mint cake on sale at the shop at Gawthrop!

Approaching Rash Bridge those leaving Dent will have noted the changing character of the dale. Hillsides are well wooded, and the undulating outline of the hills indicates a change in the geological sequence as the road passes between Holme Fell and the twin eminences of Helms Knott, known locally as 'Tweedledum and Tweedledee'. Here, by a weir, is Rash Mill, now a joiner's shop, but formerly both a carding and spinning mill, and a corn mill. It is now the scene of some activity, undergoing renovation by a work party from the Industrial Archaeology group of Sedbergh School. On a recent visit I found the lads replacing the wooden spokes of the mill wheel, now turning again; it is twenty-five years since it drove a shaft in the sawmill upstairs, now operated by electricity. Inside, beech teeth were being fitted into the metal frame of the inner wheel; expendable wooden pegs to engage with metal cogs on the drive shaft. A fireplace on this floor was used for drying corn stored above, which was brought down by two wooden chutes still *in situ*. Outside, among grass and debris, were the two millstones; a large bottom stone almost six feet in diameter, and a smaller and heavier upper stone. This is, of course, a long-term project, but eventually, one hopes, we shall see a reincarnation of Rash Mill. Perhaps we are only one step away from the return of the knitters, and television may yet have a part to play in 'gangin a sitting'. In the meantime the Dee, its travail of millrace and waterfall over, rejoices in its escape from the gates of Dent, and slips down through flowery meads to join the Rawthey.

IX

A SIGHT OF THE SEA

A SLIGHT MOVEMENT across the face of a shingle bank as of the
shadow of a passing finch – the merest interruption of the static
pattern of dazzling pebbles in the May sunshine – denotes once
again the presence of the demure ringed plover on the beaches
above Gressingham on the River Lune. The bird's pied breast
and mantle of soft grey brown – a cloak of invisibility – enable
her to disappear when stationary; her four freckled eggs are laid
in the merest of hollows among the shingle, and are wonderfully concealed by reason of their colouring. As in the case of
the larger oystercatcher, the main danger is from a sudden spate
of water, though eggs are normally laid where the beach is
highest.

In the plaintive pipe of this small wader, and in the flicker-
ing crescent of her outspread wings, there is a tang of salt spray
and mud-flat which is appropriate along this lower reach of
river. Here, a few miles above Lancaster, the Lune has more
than a hint of the sea about it. Laying down extensive shingle
banks, it speeds by undeterred at the thought of its forth-
coming encounter with the turmoil of industry, or of its
melancholy passage by quays long silent, before it wins the
freedom of Morecambe Bay.

At Loyne Bridge, where salmon linger and the tide has lost
its impetus, the remains of two castles lie in close proximity.
Castlestede, by the bridge, now screened by trees and vegetation, is a good example of a motte and bailey castle, and may
be of Danish or Saxon origin, while on rising ground beyond
the church and houses of Hornby village, the towers of a
nineteenth-century mansion screen the original Norman keep.
The castle has been in the successive possession of the Lonville,
Neville and Stanley families and somewhat surprisingly escaped
destruction by victorious Parliamentary troops in 1643. Other
fortified vantage points are to be found at Halton, Burton, and
Arkholme.

Now in May the way up-dale is edged with flowers. Broad

acres of dandelions, despised and brilliant, lay a carpet of incomparable gold by the roadside; jack-by-the-hedge rears a wall of pale green against burgeoning hedgerows; and cherry blossom shows white in woodland still leafless. At Hornby the widening valley gives views of Leck and Barbon Fells and the road, winding through a green and rolling countryside among knolls clothed with conifers, follows the edge of the broad flood plain. At Melling with its grey old church tower and air of Georgian elegance there is scarcely room to pass, and to the east a diaphanous halo of vapour wreathes the summit of Ingleborough – a bridal veil of light against the morning sun.

At Greta Bridge (inscribed on the parapet as Greeta) the road skirts the parkland of Thurland Castle, once the home of the Tunstall family from whom the nearby village takes its name. Sir Brian de Tunstall, less fortunate than many of the dalesmen who fought with him, was killed at Flodden in 1513. His will requested burial "in the outward part of the church of Seynt Mychaell in Tunstall"; the dedication is now to St John Baptist. During the Civil Wars Thurland was overrun by the Roundheads and dismantled. On the north side of the park, a little distance from a neat row of white cottages and an inn called The Lunesdale, stands Tunstall church with its crenellated walls and large rectangular porch. Here in a little room above the entrance the girls of the Clergy Daughters' School at Cowan Bridge, attending Tunstall church each Sunday, had their picnic lunch; among those girls in 1824 were four of the daughters of the Rev. Patrick Brontë of Haworth, a place all too far removed to four impressionable and homesick young girls. "Great grey hills heaved up around the horizon; as twilight deepened we descended a valley dark with wood, and long after night had overclouded the prospect, I heard a wild wind rushing among trees". Small wonder that Charlotte was to recall her childhood aversion to the hard, grey hills of Craven and Lunesdale when twenty years later she wrote *Jane Eyre*; Cowan Bridge school became 'Lowood', and Tunstall, 'Brocklebridge'.

Charlotte's "great grey hills" were nothing short of delectable as I made my way past cottage gardens gay with aubretia and wallflowers to Tunstall church, venerable among fading daffodils. There were enchanting views of Gragareth and Ingleborough, blue-domed, through a vignette of pink cherry;

patches of delicate blue at the foot of the tower proved to be germander speedwell of a particularly light-petalled variety.

The chancel floor of Dent marble, the recumbent knightly effigy, and the remains of a votive stone to Asclepius and Hygieia inside the building seemed strangely in keeping with this pleasant corner of English countryside, for the early life of the valley was very much bound up with the comings and goings of the Romans during the three hundred years of their presence. Coins and pavements found in the area are linked with the fort at Burrow (Overborough), established in A.D.79 by Agricola along a military highway that ran from Ribchester via Bowland and Lunesdale to the Scottish border; stretches of the modern road along the east bank of the river now follow its course. From this road at various points lanes run down to the Lune, and fords connected hamlet and village as, for example, at Arkholme and Whittington; there is no bridge along the eight miles between Hornby and Kirkby Lonsdale, where there are two within a hundred yards!

By hedges increasingly white with blackthorn blossom – all the more beautiful because of the absence of leaves – road and river draw closer together on the approach to Kirkby, constricted by the mass of the Pennines to the east, and on the other hand by the isolated scars of Hutton Roof Crag and Farleton Knott. Both these are of limestone, rising to almost 900 feet with magnificent views of Morecambe Bay and the Lakeland fells. The southern sections above Burton are well wooded; conifers are interspersed with a variety of young hardwoods, and beech and maple are prominent in autumn with brilliant splashes of copper and flame. Berries – hips, haws, guelder rose, rowan and bryony – provide more intimate interludes of colour, as do the many fungi, which last until the first frosts; the delicate purple amethyst deceiver, which flourishes in some of the higher plantations, is particularly lovely. Goldcrest, bullfinch, jay, cole tit, and marsh tit haunt the thick woodland, and on the dry hillside of Hutton Roof crag, thorn, briar, and some bracken provide cover for warbler and yellowhammer. Juniper, disappearing in many localities, is nowhere more abundant than on the summit edge. One of the most heartening sights in the wayward days of early spring, when wild daffodils begin to bloom and sun and frost alternate, is the sight of the first butterfly, a brimstone or a peacock, moving erratically across the woodland clearings.

At its northern end the limestone eminence is much more exposed; extensive pavement and outcrop, quarried on its western flank, develop into a fine scarp above the hamlet of Farleton.

Perhaps the finest vantage point on a hilltop of superlative prospects is at the south-eastern and of Newbiggin Crags, above the slopes where a network of narrow leafy lanes descend towards Kirkby Lonsdale, apparently in no hurry to get there, and where the sudden appearance of a tractor would cause traffic problems. On the scarp edge on a mad March day, ensconced among the brilliant sunlit crags, one can miss the worst of the north wind; whatever privations this icy tyrant may bring, at least they are accompanied by exceptional visibility and skies of dramatic mobility. Against a backdrop of almost thirty miles of Lunesdale, from the Howgills in the north to the dark horizontal of Clougha above Lancaster, a sky of pellucid blue is vibrant with incident. From time to time, moving columns of grey vapour, bringing snow flurries, are swept southward, obliterating all before them. There are three at work as I watch; one has wiped away the Howgills; another has laid siege to Barbon; and to the east the dome of Ingleborough is threatened. Purely local in effect, these showers are of short duration; it is merely a matter of time before one strikes my sheltered station, but above at the moment a huge billowing cumulus several miles in extent sits astride the valley. From its level base the tangible white vapour, exquisitely modelled, towers a thousand feet or more, in the afternoon sun as softly substantial in form as the hard crags beneath; the clean lines of its summit are broken where frozen filaments trail upwards towards the zenith.

It must have been under equally scenic conditions that Ruskin and Turner made the acquaintance of the Lune valley; their acclaim first established its reputation for a classic beauty that vies with Wharfedale and Fountains Abbey. "The valley of the Lune at Kirkby is one of the loveliest scenes in England, and therefore in the world. Whatever moorland hill, and sweet river, and English forest foliage can be at their best is gathered here . . ." With Ruskin's definitive pronouncement one humbly concurs.

I could never bring myself to enthuse about towns, but –
Kirkby Lonsdale is the exception; it is a place that might have
been put together by Adam, Dickens, and Pevsner, at one and
the same time. It has a bridge – the one described as "the finest
of our ancient English bridges". The one with the inscription,
"Fear God, Honor the King, 1633". An old bridge, one is
inclined to remark. But there is more. Its origin is uncertain,
but in the 1270s it was old and in need of attention, and
pontage was duly granted. Of course, you will hear the story of
the bridge – the 'Devil's Bridge' – and if you can hear it from
octogenarian Jonty Wilson, in the gloom of his blacksmith's
shop, so much the better, for Jonty's memory, like the bridge
and the Devil, go back a long way in time. Writer, traveller,
local historian, blacksmith, broadcaster, soldier, photographer,
and doyen of the Dales, there is not much he has not done. We
looked at his collection of picture-postcards; Jonty, pale-faced
beneath a battered trilby, commentated. One picture of a
young giant in athlete's garb prompted a question.

"It's me," replied Jonty, in his soft clear voice. "Ah won
t'mile race at Dent sports in 1913."

The last time I saw the old man he looked very tired.
Television has made its claims on Jonty, and it is a long ride to
the studios in Manchester.

The legend of the old bridge has many versions; one,
expressed in rhyme, and written a century and a half ago by a
poet called Whalley, begins

> Still grand and beautiful, and good,
> Has Lonsdale bridge unshaken stood
> And scorned the swollen raging flood –
> For many ages.

The story concerns "an old maid, queer in her ways, in
Yorkshire bred", who, sacrificing her dog on the bridge,
cheated the Devil of her own soul. The poem ends with an
exhortation to the "dwellers on its banks":-

> Be faithful each to Church and King.
> And cheat the devil.

Before the building of the modern bridge which connects
with Main Street, the old coach road entered by Devil's Bridge,
and Mill Brow, which leads to The Sun Inn and The King's

Arms, the latter dating from the sixteenth century. Extra horses were hitched on to coaches at the foot of the steep hill, which would be particularly bad to negotiate in winter. No doubt one of the jobs of the ostler's lads would be to prepare and scatter sand from the river bed on the slippery slope; another would be to carry ale to thirsty bell ringers at the church, at the cost of the parish! Kirkby is well served with inns – formerly there were twenty-nine – and at The Sun it was traditional for the landlord to read aloud the London News sheet. Water mills, now houses, above the river, once produced carpets, snuff and bone, and were powered by an artificial mill race that ran from Beck Head and beneath Market Street, where on either hand are the Horsemarket and the Swine-market, now accommodating the old market cross; from here a narrow 'ginnel' leads to the churchyard, and to 'Ruskin's View' – a splendid panorama of river and fells. The present church dates from about 1100, and has a fine Norman archway and six ponderous dissimilar capitals of the same period, near the west door. There is an air of dignity and elegance in the tall crenellated tower and low-pitched roof of this ancient parish church to which the part-Georgian vicarage, wrought-iron gates, and old-world cottages add their own contribution. The churchyard has all the atmosphere of a cathedral precinct, enhanced, according to season, by snowdrop, crocus, daffodil, rose and Virginia creeper; Ruskin himself, with all his aesthetic nicety, could not have chosen a more beautiful setting for his favourite view.

Beyond the gazebo and the vicarage, the green mound of Cockpit Hill – the name tells its own story – a green mound backed by trees is the site of yet another of Lunesdale's motte and baileys, recalling the days when Thane Torfin held sway in 'Cherkeby Lownesdale'. A mile and a half to the north, on land originally granted to the Norman Ughtred, stands Underley Hall, rebuilt in the 1820s, and the property of, among others, the Earl of Bective, and the Cavendish-Bentinck family.

Across the river, Casterton village, once on the course of the Roman road to Overborough, and now a cluster of roof tops set among a maze of leafy byways, will, perhaps, best be re-membered for its Brontë associations. The famous girls' school founded by the Rev. William Carus Wilson originally for clergy daughters was brought here from Cowan Bridge in 1833.

There are many wild and lovely valleys that run down to Lunesdale from the east, draining the high fells of Middleton, Barbon and Gragareth. The latter and its neighbour Crag Hill (2,239 feet) give rise to Easegill, a long valley between Leck Fell and Brownthwaite. The mere mention of 'Leck' or 'Easegill' is enough to kindle the lamp of any member of the potholing fraternity, for whom the limestone sections of these hills have become a Mecca; there are none to dispute the appeal of the Easegill and Lancaster Hole systems, for length of passage and spectacular formations. To a Philistine who, like myself, can seldom find sufficient time to explore the countryside above the ground, the ways of the pot-holer may seem inexplicable. "Wet clothes for a few hours are delightful ..." "... the comprehensive, poetic-sensuous appeal of caves ..." The foregoing passages are from the excellent writings of David Heap, master speliologist, who, with a puzzling juxtaposition of sensations, thus extols the virtues of caving. Perhaps it is all part of the paradox of those who seek the wide open spaces in order to commit themselves to restrictive darkness and the esoteric appeal of the underworld. We are reminded by Cadoux that "it was from caves that men stepped out to discover themselves". Whatever reservations are held about pot-holing, one has to have regard for men who can express such sentiments. Their technical language is, incidentally, completely incomprehensible – perhaps directly from the Anglo-Saxon; repeat the following quickly, and you will gather what I mean: "Pitch, choke, aven, gour, sump!"

They will understand you all right up at Bull Pot Farm, under Crag Hill, where a notice on the door of the main building announces 'Red Rose Cave and Potholing Club'. The title and painted emblem on the wall remind one that here a long triangle of Lancashire projects into foreign (Yorkshire) territory. A further notice wishes you 'A Happy Birthday – with Maltesers'. In spite of this display of affability, the door is locked. Gone fishing? – Gone to earth, more likely! And you can take your pick of Bull Pot of the Witches, Cow Pot, Lancaster Hole, Top Sink, County Pot, and so on; many of them are considerably more obvious on the sketch map hung in the porch than they are in real life. Across the valley, where the "loneliest farm in Lancashire" (one of the many!) looks up at the Three Men of Gragareth, are Rumbling Hole, Death's Head Hole, and Lost John's Cave.

I have seen Leck Fell in many moods, but never so benevolent as on the May morning when, having negotiated the network of lanes around Casterton, I breast Brownthwaite and drop down towards Gale Garth, pausing for refreshment by an outcrop atop steep bracken slopes. A movement among the dead fronds presently reveals itself as a ring ouzel, foraging among the cover. As he hops out the white gorget is plainly visible. Almost simultaneously the song of a blackbird is heard from a copse by the streamside; at this height of a thousand feet, the breeding range of the two birds overlaps, though there are minor differences in the nest and eggs of these kindred species. The ring ouzel usually nests in a crag or gully, often among heather, and the deep staccato of his alarm notes, like large pebbles knocked together, is quite distinctive. Towards the end of July both birds will be found among the bilberries.

In the distance, the cluster of buildings at Bull Pot Farm shows clearly, as yet unscreened among ash and sycamore still bare. A lonely spot, but the swallows find it; they arrived a fortnight ago. When one thinks of all the cosy old barns of the dale standing four square among flowers, with Vacant Possession . . . But sentiment in wild nature is misplaced; to the swallows of Bull Pot, corrugated iron takes precedence over cowslips.

From the slopes of Brownthwaite the nature of the terrain is clearly demonstrated; heather slopes giving way to unbroken grassland at the head of the dale; as in Kingsdale, green intake is minimal. The great gash of Ease Gill, tracing a serpentine course, descends from Great Coum in a series of green knolls to join Leck Beck a stone's-throw from its resurgence; here water from the many cave systems emerges in some volume from a hole in the rock – an instant river. Indeed, this is one of the paradoxes of Easegill; a considerable chasm, it makes little contribution to Leck Beck, in normal times. One approaches it by Hellot Scales barn over grassy knolls, with the sound of waterfalls in the main beck close by. A sudden descent reveals the depth of Ease Gill, carved down into the limestone of the hillside. A path follows the edge on either hand, but access along the river bed, blocked by pools of clearest water, is difficult or impossible. For the most part the ravine is dry, though all the signs are of the erstwhile presence of a torrent; the deeply gouged channel, moulded rocks, and damp walls have a curious sobering effect upon the senses, but the stream itself is missing. One feels like leaving a note: "I called, but you were out!" At one point there is the echoing drip of water, as the path, turning a corner, discloses a hollow vault, overhung by ash and rowan, and passes precariously above a circular fissure partly filled with water. The sides of the gill, rising like the fluted columns of a cathedral, are surmounted by a tracery of branches – a green clerestory through which the light filters; in a week or so, when the leaves have expanded, Ease Gill Kirk will celebrate the feast of high summer with additional solemnity. One remembers the brass band festivals at Hardraw, and tries to imagine the effect of a choral mass in Ease Gill; for the moment the sound of the human voice here in the Kirk would seem irreverent.

From Bull Pot Farm two grass tracks diverge. One, wet and stony, peters out on the rushy slopes of Crag Hill; the other, broad and inviting, leads down to Barbondale by Aygill, a delightful beck that would seem more at home in the Lake District, having more than its fair share of waterfalls, rowans, and bracken. A further affinity with Lakeland is found in the changing profile of the hills to the north, which are ruggedly undulating, for here the Dent fault, angled against the Craven fault lines, has caused a major dislocation. A ribbon of road climbs gently up-dale, its gradual incline in contrast with the violent scarp slope of Middleton Fell; the view from the summit of the pass into Dentdale is one that should be lingered over.

On its west bank the Lune is fringed by more modest hills, which undulate pleasantly northward. Some of the heights are crowned with heather; on others, there are tarns that lie in hollows, mirroring the trees that ring them, and the changing skies – Terry Bank with its coot and tufted duck; Windymere and its flowers; Kitmere, above Rigmaden, encircled by rhododendrons and noisy with gulls. Through this rolling country-side roads gravitate towards Kendal, or drop down eventually, perhaps by Old Town and Killington, towards Sedbergh. On the east bank of the river there are few hamlets beyond Barbon, and these, like the roads, are squeezed down into the valley by the mass of Middleton Fell (1,942 feet). Not far from the river, at Hawking Hall, a cylindrical Roman milestone that came to light in 1836 has been re-erected in a field; Collingwood calls the relic "the best in the country". Agricola's legions, too, trod this same lowland route to the Lune gorge. Close by, a fourteenth-century mansion was the home for over three hundred years of the Middleton family. The remains of court-yards, archway, and banqueting hall can still be seen, despite the damage done by Cromwell's cannon-balls, and the ravages of time.

By Middleton Bridge the Lune receives the combined waters of the rivers Clough, Dee and Rawthey, and in this green enclosed triangle of land stands Ingmire Hall, once the seat of the Upton and Otway families. Those whose atten-tion is on Ingmire, or who are unduly anxious to complete the last mile into Sedbergh, will miss the narrow road that leads down to the Rawthey, a lane too confined, fortunate-ly, to accommodate cars. I shall not forget my first visit to the Quaker Meeting House at Brigflatts, at the end of a long journey on an exquisite May morning. A group of buildings shaded by trees marked the end of the lane. One house, large and gracious, had a date stone 'A.I.E. 1743', and across the way a smaller cottage, very neat, very white, hid itself away, almost apologetically, behind a bank of honesty and primroses. Its mullioned windows looked out on to an old-world garden, overhung by yews, with a view beyond of more flowers – forget-me-nots, tulips, and lilies-of-the-valley. One cannot imagine a more charming place. As I hesitated, lost in admiration, a Scottish voice greeted me from the doorway, and bade me enter. In the solid stone porch, above an alcove with a posy of flowers, the date 'A.D. 1675' caught my eye, and a half-open, iron-studded door gave a glimpse of an interior with white walls and old woodwork. Later, on a seat in the garden, I listened to the story of the house. Mr McGregor, the custodian, is no mean story-teller – a man with a gentle voice and the lilting inflection of Dr Finlay! One remembers Brigflatts as a haven of peace and learning, where, apparently, even the rabbits are literate! On a small notice in one of the flower beds of the inner garden I read:

Mr McGregor's Garden,
No Rabbits.
By Order.

To describe Brigflatts in springtime there is no other word but idyllic.

X

THE HOWGILLS

TRAVELLERS to Scotland by the M6 may on seeing the Lune gorge persuade themselves that they have already reached the Highlands. For here, along the most scenic stretch of motorway between London and the border, the Howgills manifest a landscape that is more of Cairngorm than Pennine. Although only half the height of their Highland counterpart, this massif has many similarities: a raised plateau with several summits and outlying spurs, and overall, a symmetry of outline absent from the ridge and scarp upland to the south and east. In the case of the Howgills, however, its rock outcrops are insignificant, and are confined to steeper gills and to something of a corrie wall at Cautley; it is lacking in spectacular *arêtes,* but is superlative walking country. Of its many summits around the 2,000 foot contour line, the Calf (2,220 feet) takes precedence, and is the focal point from which most of its valleys radiate. In the north and west drainage is directly into the Lune; elsewhere, the Rawthey gathers most of its streams, which are short and swift, and descend by steeply cut gills. Those at Black Force and Cautley are particularly spectacular. Drystone walling is minimal – an unusual feature on the Pennines – and the flowing symmetrical outlines and smooth rounded flanks, almost feminine in aspect, are best appreciated under a low sun. The geological affinities of the Howgills, separated from the Askrigg Block by the valley of Rawthey, are with the slates of southern Lakeland. It is hardly surprising that these hills, with their beauty of form, have endeared themselves to those who have lived among them, like the generations of boys of Sedbergh's famous school, whose traditional anthem 'Winder', named after a spur of the Howgills, speaks of the "memory ... of Winder's clear cut outline, against an evening sky". One of the school's most renowned old boys was the geologist Adam Sedgwick, who from Firbank used to admire the view of "five distinct valleys which seemed to unite in a great basin or central depression"; he ends by exhorting his fellows to "warm their hearts by gazing over this cluster of noble dales ... the home of their childhood".

Firbank rises to a thousand feet above the gorge of the Lune, and gives a grandstand view of the western wall of the Howgills; it is "easily reached", as the guide-books would say, from The Black Horse on the Sedbergh road, or from the old road to Tebay. On the December day I first 'discovered' Firbank, the ascent was anything but easy. Frost and overnight snow have a habit of making the easiest of climbs into an arduous and difficult task, and it was not without relief that I reached the Knotts, a rocky knoll showing dark on the leeward face. There was certainly plenty to admire. Across the dale in alternating segments of white snow and blue shadow, the deeply grooved spurs of Winder, Arant Haw, and White Fell projected above the valley floor. Half an hour later, an incredible change brought driving snow, and reduced visibility to a few yards. Muffled against the blizzard, I groped my way off the summit, slithering down a steep bank towards a stunted larch that overhung a drystone wall. The vague outlines of an enclosure of some sort loomed up; even a sheep-fold has its merits, under such conditions, and I was glad to crouch behind a wall and escape the worst of the blast. For a spell the snow did its best to obliterate my retreat, piling itself against every projection in its path; presently, through the whirligig of snowflakes, there came a sudden light in the sky, veiled at first, then brilliant as the sun broke through, revealing every aspect of my surroundings. The enclosure proved to be larger than anticipated, and at the far side a stone slab encased in white leaned over into the elements. Brushing my gloved hand across its surface, I perceived a faint inscription beneath the snow, and the date 1800. As I moved towards a gap in the far wall, I realized that I had had four companions in the blizzard. Two were sheep, which rose from behind an outcrop in one corner, and made off, rattling like bead curtains, their fleeces hung with icicles. My other two companions were less demonstrative. I left William and Elizabeth Beetham, silent guardians of that lonely and elevated spot, to keep their vigil as they had done for almost two centuries on the hallowed ground where once stood Firbank old church.

The church, destroyed by a gale in 1839, was originally Roman Catholic, but under the Cromwellian dispensation became Presbyterian. It was so when George Fox came to it to preach on a Sunday morning in June 1652. Arriving on Firbank later than expected, and finding the church filled to overflowing, he addressed the multitude from the vantage point of a nearby outcrop, watched by others of his followers from the church windows. For three hours he discoursed, and his visit is recorded on a plaque set on a rock face close to the wall of the overgrown graveyard: " 'Let your lives speak'. Here or near this rock George Fox preached to about one thousand seekers for three hours ... great power inspired his message, and the meeting proved of first importance in gathering the Society of Friends known as Quakers."

From Vernon Noble we have a glimpse of the magnetic evangelist.

Wearing a large white hat, his hair in ringlets to his shoulders, a long plain jacket and the leather breeches with which he was to be identified by the crowds, he plodded the country lanes from town to town, preaching, praying and protesting ... A tribute to his cleanliness, in spite of sleeping out and being thrown into ponds and ditches by angry crowds, was paid by a Yorkshire magistrate who said he could tell by his linen he was not a vagrant.

The dalesfolk, mainly farmers and artisans, who flocked to listen to Fox's message found his words much to their liking, and the Quaker influence spread throughout the north, being particularly strong in Swaledale and around Sedbergh. Meetings were held in private houses and in the open air, many of the Friends suffering persecution for failure to attend their parish church, or for non-payment of tithes; in 1660, of some five hundred 'Seekers' imprisoned at York, many were local folk. It is said that one dalesman never attended a meeting without taking his night-cap, in case he was apprehended and sent off to gaol. Gatherings were held at Grayrigg, at Garsdale, and in the valley of Lune at Brigflatts, where in 1674 land was bought for a meeting house. This was built as a co-operative effort, and on one occasion in 1677 was attended by more than five hundred people, including George Fox and his wife. Today, the neat little cottage set among lilacs and lilies-of-the-valley peeps out across the Rawthey with an unassuming grace that befits the second oldest meeting house in England. A stone pinnacle on a column on the lawn is a fragment of Sedbergh market-cross, destroyed in 1854 – a memento of the visit to the town of the Quaker, William Dewsbury. Inside the porch a heavy iron-studded door opens into a large single room, galleried on three sides, with oak benches, balustrades, and flooring. A wooden gate gives access to a staircase that creaks as one ascends to the gallery. From here, by a small library, one looks down into a room not unlike a courthouse, complete with railed rostrum. To this pleasant scene add sunlight streaming through mullioned windows on to white walls and dark oak, clean and almost clinical, and the softer radiance of a bowl of jonquils set in the middle of the room; through the window the outline of Holme Fell is picked out in the sunshine. In the quiet garden one reflects, perhaps, on the forces which down the centuries have manipulated the lives of the dalesfolk – Scottish raiders, poverty, reformer, railway – and one wonders if ever a latter-day Fox will bring them crowding again into the narrow lane at Brigflatts. But today, it seems, the 'seekers' arrive in caravans, and the current evangelism is that of the motor-car and television. Behind the screen of yews and sunlit garden, the world moves on its way towards Sedbergh, and in a room across the lane they are watching the Cup Final.

From the heights of Firbank the courses of the many becks that carve their way from the western slopes of the Howgills can be plainly seen, sometimes flanked with trees, or with loose lines of farmsteads – Fairmile, Chapel, and Croasdale Becks. Hedgerows and narrow lanes pattern the lower hillside, where a pack-horse track from Kendal once traversed the fells to Ravenstonedale and Kirkby Stephen, crossing the Lune at Hole Ford and climbing by Chapel Beck. On the hillside a curiously shaped dark patch of stones and vegetation assumes the shape of a large animal; you will have to look twice at the Horse of Busha' (Bush Howe) for it has not been groomed for many years, and in its prime was never a Derby winner. Formerly, it was given an annual 'spring clean' by local folk, to preserve its figure, but now it has gone the way of all flesh and, ample of rump and long-necked, looks sadly towards Sedbergh.

Chapel Beck has made its own contribution to local history. John Blaykling, the Quaker friend with whom George Fox stayed on the occasion of his visit to Brigflatts, lived at Draw Well, a venerable farmstead in Bland. As its name implies, it had a never-failing supply of water, and in the adjoining barn the Friends used to meet. It was from here that George Fox travelled to preach at Firbank on that memorable day in June 1677, when he addressed his followers in the open air; the spot on the fell is still known as 'Fox's Pulpit'.

At Howgill, in a pleasant green hollow, the little parish church stands precariously by a beck given to flooding. At this simple towerless building with its many tall lancet windows, local folk attend an annual lambing-service. On a May morning I watched the dalesfolk arrive, carrying baskets of refreshments for this special occasion. Inside, I was welcomed to a church surprisingly bright and airy, with pews of light coloured wood, and a red carpet; above the door one notices the following exhortation: "Whosoever thou art that enterest this church, leave it not without one prayer to God for thyself, for them who minister, and those who worship here."

Now the final hymn, led by a single white-haired dalesman. "That's old Tom Sedgwick. 'E's eighty-three, and 'e's bin in't choir for ower sixty year!" a parishioner informs me. Outside on the grass a Swaledale ewe is penned, along with her two lambs: "Wi call 'em Gert and Daisy – they're gimmers!" The minister quits his congregation, and moves out to the pen. Rain is falling steadily, but the blessing is pronounced. The sheep look unconcerned, but the onlookers are moved to unpack their baskets, and tea is served; another dales year completes its cycle. In this most peaceful of settings it seems incredible that the few cottages and derelict woollen mill close by once catered for an industry that employed more than a hundred people, and kept a carter fully occupied ferrying its products to Kendal, the centre of the knitting industry. There were, of course, many other mills in the area, drawing their power from hill streams, and recruiting their labour force mainly from women and children. The Sedbergh mills at Farfield and Rawthey Bank turned out horse cloths; that at Hebblethwaite Hall produced yarn for cottage knitters. The latter mill was built in 1792 by the Quaker Robert Forster to help the poor, who were also provided with a school. Knitted hose, gloves and caps were produced in thousands, and were, according to Defoe, "very coarse and ordinary". These were taken to market by pack horse along traditional grass tracks, or by carrier as roads improved; at the close of the eighteenth century over 800 pairs of stockings were taken each week from

Sedbergh and Dent to Kendal, providing employment for about 120 wool combers. Prior to the introduction of the Spinning Jenny about 1770, the spinning of yarn had been part of a cottage industry, and one or two spinning galleries, where the spinning wheels could stand and be operated under cover and in good light, are still to be seen; there is a good example at Adamthwaite, and another at Railton Yard, in Sedbergh. A stone's-throw away, the name of Weavers' Yard recalls the days when Sedbergh's first weaving looms were set up here in a cobbled courtyard. Cotton mills at Birks and Millthrop, like others, failed, and were adapted to other purposes. Many such buildings became bobbin or sawmills, and currently are being modified for domestic purposes and sold to 'off-comers' from the towns.

One mill which has so far escaped the attentions of the 'developer' lies in a rocky gill at Davy Bank, close to Crook o' Lune Bridge. Sitting in the garden there at Mill House, one hears the perpetual sound of water; upstream, hidden in a wooded gorge, a number of small cataracts pour down across slabs of rock colourful in spring with the rich greens of golden saxifrage and wood sorrel. Stopping one day to look at a dipper's nest under the mill bridge, I came upon Elsie Middleton washing a brush and rods in the beck; she had just swept her own chimney. At Mill House they are independent, and until recent years made their own electricity. She needed no telling about the dipper's nest, having watched the bird from her front window. "Ah went to loowk under t'bridge," Elsie explained, "but ah cudna' git to it 'cus mi welly were full o'wahter." There were, in fact, two nests with eggs under the arch, one having been immersed in flood water earlier in the season, and spoilt. No wonder the Middletons' 'home-made' electricity used to fluctuate before they installed a generator! I spoke to her husband Ernest, now retired, who had turned to haulage after the closure of his mill. "Ah've lived i'Mill House for nigh on seventy years, an' ah've nivver regretted a minit of it," the soft-spoken dalesman told me. "Ah've ground many a ton o'corn, speshly oats an' barley, till t'wheel split i'two, an' that were twenty years ago."

The town of Sedbergh lies at the foot of the southern tip of the Howgills, on the lower slopes of Winder and Crook and close to the River Rawthey where the mills of Birks and

Millthrop once flourished. Behind the town, on Castlehaw, a green mound is all that remains of a Norman motte and bailey castle, a fortified viewpoint which could dominate approaches across the river, and by road, for Sedbergh has always been a centre of communication, lying on cross-country routes from Kendal to Lancaster, and from Lakeland to Wensleydale. In the second half of the eighteenth century roads were improved, and toll bars can still be seen along many of the modern highways, as at Borrett Bar, on the southern approaches to the town. The early stage-coaches running between Lancaster and Newcastle from the 1820s onwards called at the Market Place, halting outside The King's Arms, now a shop.

It is recorded that on one occasion, in the early hours of a frosty morning in midwinter, the mail coach left for Kirkby Stephen with three men and a woman riding inside. Some miles further on, at The Cross Keys at Cautley (now a Temperance Inn), the driver and one passenger got out for a drink. A few minutes later the horses started off of their own accord, and minus driver and passenger, negotiated the abominable road to Kirkby Stephen, where the remainder of the passengers descended for refreshment. Shortly afterwards the missing traveller arrived on horseback to find the coach and horses safely drawn up outside The King's Arms; there is no mention of what happened to the driver!

As in the case of so many dales towns, different eras of history are well represented. From the slopes of Winder one can look down on Sedbergh and note the various stages of its growth. An examination of place-names in the area will reveal a strong Norse influence; 'setberg' means flat-topped hill, and it is probable that the original settlement may have been below Castlehaw. The oldest part of the present town lies around the church and market place, extending down Main Street, where a shop with an overhanging upper storey, originally early seventeenth century, can still be seen; behind the narrow street, yards and cottages were built. Railton Yard, with its deserted cottages and spinning gallery, squeezed into a grey stone backwater, offers a glimpse of the past – an incredible film-set of dereliction and dandelions, unexpectedly quiet on this May morning except for the screaming of swifts. Round the corner, on the steps of Lupton House, an annexe of Sedbergh School, a bevy of youths lounge in the sunshine enjoying their tea break;

from indoors comes the sound of a transistor. A helpful lad from Chester, busy with a slice of jam and bread, pauses for a moment to chat, and points out the way to Weavers' Yard, where a seventeenth-century external chimney breast is reputed to have been the hiding place of Bonnie Prince Charlie. The chimney is at the rear of what is now a chemist's shop, and is part of the former town house of the Upton family. Hand looms in Weavers' Yard once wove a narrow coarse cloth called 'Kerseys', and checks used for horse collars. The materials were then taken to Hebblethwaite Hall mill for washing and fulling.

A thriving woollen industry in the mid nineteenth century brought an increase in population, and housing extended on the north-west of the town. Many houses resemble those of Lakeland in style, and the Old Vicarage beyond the playing fields has the seventeenth-century 'barrel' chimneys which are sometimes a feature of older Cumbrian farmhouses.

Sedbergh is perhaps best known for its school – "the most prominent school in the north of England". Founded in 1525 by Dr Roger Lupton, the chantry partly survived the Dissolution to become a free grammar school, from which developed the present school complex. The oldest part, on the road to Dent, dates from 1716 and is now a library and museum. The school's students have included many famous men, including the mathematician John Dawson, scientist James Inman, and geologist Adam Sedgwick.

North-east of Sedbergh, the Rawthey, turning sharply from its birthplace on Baugh Fell, follows the course of the trunk road from Newcastle to the Lancashire coast. Swift-flowing over its rocky bed, with numerous waterfalls, and overlooked by the steeply plunging spurs of Knott, Middle Tongue, and Ben End, the river pursues its turbulent course towards the Lune, its beauty enhanced by the addition of smaller streams that join it from spectacular gills and coombs. At Cautley, a wall of dark rock crumbles over a hollow corrie, and a white thread of water, visible a mile away from the road, leaps down a gash in the hillside. Seen from the precipitous slopes of its edge Cautley Spout is an impressive spot, though at times the narrow chasm with rowans springing from the very brink can be an uncomfortable perch, and one is likely to be drenched with upflung spray. Ravens and buzzards are a frequent sight about the crag, but when soaring and wheeling at some height above the corrie are sometimes difficult to distinguish one from the other. The voice is, of course, conclusive. The 'cronking' of the raven and the cat-like 'mewing' of the buzzard are quite dissimilar; the former bird has a habit, too, of sudden wing closing, and rolling in the air. Climbing quietly up the gorge one February day, I came suddenly face to face with a heron, fishing in a pool at the foot of one stage of the waterfall. Trapped thus in the hollow of rocks, the bird had great difficulty in rising and turning, but after a moment of in-decision, presented me with a splendid close-up of its outspread wings, and broke free. A special bonus at Cautley is the occasional sighting of a peregrine.

The becks that join the Rawthey hereabouts from the wall of the Howgills are short and tumultuous, but on the northern side a series of long valleys drain towards the infant Lune, which rises above Newbiggin on Green Bell. Close by is the source of Scandal Beck, and the lonely farmhouse of Adamthwaite, accessible from the Cautley side by Scot's Rake, a steep path which climbs northward over the watershed. Otherwise this isolated farmstead, with its spinning gallery and sheltering trees, is reached by a long and hazardous road from the valley of Ravenstonedale.

Near Artlebeck, Tom Nicholson farms at Shaw Mire. "Wi've Rough Fell sheep, and sucklin' cows, and a few fell ponies," he told me. "Thi'r good enough to sell, is 'osses, like; wi gen'lly tek oors t' t'Hawes."

I commented on the remoteness of the place, and the possibility of stock being stolen.

"Aw! Wi've got a policeman in't villige. 'E's got a dog a' two, a pony and trap, and a gote and a young 'un; 'e's a grand lad, is oor copper!"

In the days when men were hunters rather than farmers, Ravenstonedale was forest land. Today the village lies in a pleasant hollow green with cultivation and set among orderly rectangles of good walling. There is, nevertheless, more than a hint of wildness in the magnificent skyline of surrounding fells, where deer and boar once roamed, for Ravenstonedale's affinities are with the Eden and Mallerstang – and who could conjure up names more wild and primitive than those?

A feature of the Middle Ages was the dale's system of justice,

the 'peculiar Court of Ravenstonedale', which was administered by the Lord of the Manor and a Grand Jury of twenty-
four local men of integrity. These exercised supreme power in
the area, from the imposition of the death sentence to trivial
fines. Eavesdroppers were fined 6s. 8d.; for quarrels in the
churchyard, 3s. 4d.; and "any person playing football within
the precincts of this lordship shall be fined 12d.". Obviously the
game had caught on in the days of Good Queen Bess! Less
trivial was the gibbet on Gallows Hill in the deer-park, where
condemned murderers were hanged. Possibly the name 'Ravenstonedale' derives from the presence of the dark scavenger at
this place of execution; as Halliwell Sutcliffe once wrote,
"names are the nursery of deeds". Or perhaps this explanation
is too facile, for it is often a mistake to accept place-names at
their face value. Perchance in Ravenstonedale we recall the
name of some Norse settler known to his fellows as 'Rafen'.

The present church of St Oswald, with a through porch
affording twin views of the extensive graveyard, dates only
from 1744, and it is noted for its three-decker pulpit and
inward facing pews, possibly for use as a court house. An older
church on the same site had a tower with a 'refuge bell',
where fugitives from the law could, by sounding this, invoke
sanctuary; they were then subject to trial in a local court.

In the mid seventeenth century the dale began an association
with the Wharton family which lasted for over a hundred
years, and it was Lord Wharton who directed his tenants to
enclose a deer park there with a wall nine feet high. Cottage
knitting was common and there were knitting schools for
children, like Dolly Coupland's in the Back Lane. Almost
everyone knitted, and their products, usually stockings, were
taken to local markets, like the one at Kirkby Stephen; a
pack-horse track crosses the Howgills and the Lune, and
connected the dale with Kendal. At the market the stockings
were sold to hosiers, who supplied the villagers with yarn for
more. Ravenstonedale was the leading district in production,
with an estimated weekly output of a thousand pairs; the
smallest size of stocking for children brought as little as 18d. for
a dozen pairs. One or two houses still have the remains of
spinning galleries, as at Newbiggin on Lune. This tiny village
of grey and white-fronted houses, often joined together, or to a
barn, is full of odd little corners. Stone steps lead to upper

storeys and enclosed yards where cattle might once have been penned suggest the days of Scottish raids across the border. Little carefree patches of garden, blessedly untidy, seem to have wandered out from cottage precincts, and wallflowers and grape hyacinths mingle with ebullient dandelion hordes. Against a hazy outline of fells a row of white-washed houses at Betsy Croft adjoins a barn, and in the angle, the tiniest of wooden spinning galleries, no more than eight or nine feet long, with stone steps, is tucked away beneath projecting eaves.

One of the best-known families of the dale is that of the Fothergills, one of whom served as standard-bearer to the first Lord Wharton at Solway Moss in 1542. The large house at Brownber, close to Newbiggin, was a residence of the family after their move from the Tarn House at Laithwaite on the Sedbergh road. This old house with its mullioned windows and neglected air bears on its porch a datestone 'G.F. - I.F. 1664'; and above, the coat of arms of the Fothergills - 'vert, a stag's head couped within a bordure inverted'. There are stories of a haunted room, and in 1877 the Rev. Nicholls of Ravenstone-dale wrote of seeing two bullet holes in a door and sword marks on the lintel, said to be the results of a fracas with a highwayman. Mrs Wyman, the present tenant, told me that visitors still come to look for these. "But," she added smiling, "Ah con see nowt misel'!" West of Ravenstonedale a number of remote dales open to the north; the dale head of Weasdale is blocked by Randygill (2,047 feet); Bowderdale is long and straight. Other valleys - Langdale, Uldale, and Ellergill - cut back deeply into the heart of the Howgills, and make their own contribution to the renowned salmon waters of the Lune, here flowing between remodelled banks, undoubtedly more efficient, but far less attractive.

XI

HEAD OF THE YORE

THOSE WHO LOVE wild flowers will find much to enthuse about in summer in Wensleydale: scabious and melancholy thistle for those who arrive by way of Bishopdale; grass of Parnassus and thrift by Aysgarth; harebells along the road to Buttertubs. By the Ure, on a dull day, golden ragwort brings its own sunlight to the river bank; foxglove, bellflower and cranesbill add colour to the byways of Coverdale. Vetch, betony, knapweed, ragged robin, in number beyond contemplation; in the grounds of Jervaulx alone over a hundred species have been recorded in a single season.

The flora of Wensleydale is as varied as one might expect in a dale of such extent, from the luxuriant poppies of Masham's cornfields to the sandwort and stonecrop of the high quarries at Redmire. Altitude and extremes of climate also have their effect in this dale of broad acres. One day in August, on a sunny afternoon drowsy with the hum of insects, I paused to admire the riot of marjoram on the ruins at Jervaulx. Meanwhile, twenty miles up-dale at Hawes shoppers were retreating across wet pavements into a lighted market-hall as a ponderous grey cloud edged its way over Stag's Fell and, reaching out over Semerwater, brought heavy rain. Is there any colour more beautiful than the delicately-elusive blue of meadow cranesbill seen beneath an overcast sky?

Richard Jefferies might have had the field paths of the Dales in mind when he wrote: "It is not only what you actually see along the path, but what you remember to have seen, that gives it its beauty". To the flower-lover, Wensleydale is a place of pilgrimage, for nowhere in the Pennines are landscape and flora more diversified, reflecting the geological structure which has produced the greenest and most spacious of all the dales. Here, the Great Scar limestone, so prominent up to about 1,200 feet in the landscape of Craven, has in its incline eastward dipped to the valley floor. Above it a rhythmic series of rocks, which Professor Phillips described as the 'Yoredales', form the sides of the dale, occurring in a sequence of thin, delicate limestone, shales, and sandstones. It is the Yoredales, with their thicker beds of the latter rock, that are responsible for the steps and terraces seen in a succession of distinctively scarped hills from Abbotside (1,756 feet), Yorburgh (1,686 feet) and Addleborough (1,564 feet) to Penhill (1,792 feet). Seen as one descends from Widdale to Hawes, Wensleydale impresses with its greenness and spaciousness, as scarps succeed each other, sometimes prefacing heights of over two thousand feet, yet never oppressive, such is the extent of the level valley floor, along which the Ure meanders, mile after mile. Villages grace its course, or sit on terraces on the hillside, with their satellite hamlets and out-barns. Woodland follows the contour lines, or climbs steeply up the scarps, gouged with gills and waterfalls, as at Hardraw, Cotter Force, and above Askrigg. Grass tracks climb into the intimacy of side dales of whose number one loses count; good roads over England's highest passes, like Fleet Moss (1,934 feet) and Buttertubs (1,726 feet), connect with Wharfedale and Swaledale, and peat and heather moors on grit and sandstone heights add their own contribution to a dales landscape of unaccustomed grandeur. Comparisons with other dales are unsatisfactory, though its moorland may have a touch of Nidderdale. The green of its fields and trees is richer than the delicate ash greens of Malham or Wharfedale, its scarps more restrained. Ribblesdale has something of its greenness and vastness, of its breadth of view, but it lacks side dales. Both have suffered, and benefited, from, the incursion of a 'through' railway line which encouraged industries like quarrying and milk production, and, certainly in the case of Wensleydale, brought about economic stability in an era of depopulation when lead and textiles declined.

A feature observed in so many other dales is the change in character beyond a certain point; in Wensleydale, it occurs at Askrigg, which marked the edge of the medieval forest. Below this, castle, monastery, fortified house, and parkland are features of a widening valley with increasing arable land. Up-dale, place names (may) recall the Norse farmers who under the Normans were forced to turn to keeping cows and pigs when their settlements became forest-lodges, and sheep grazing was restricted. 'Forests' - not necessarily wooded - were wild areas preserved for hunting, where landowners, in this case the lords of Richmond and Wensleydale, exercised Forest Laws. In the Forest of Wensley, which extended as far as Mallerstang, lodges were established at Appersett, Countersett, Burtersett, and Lunds, and at a headquarters in Bainbridge, twelve foresters were appointed.

The Ure, or Yore, winding its way through a comparatively straight valley, at least as far as Aysgarth, is bounded on the north by the commons of Abbotside and Askrigg, and by the moors of Bolton, Preston and Bellerby. On the south side, high ground includes Widdale Fell (2,203 feet), and Dodd Fell (2,189 feet), Wether Fell (2,015 feet) Addleborough and Penhill. From its birthplace in Sails (2,186 feet) the infant Ure ('Jor', to the monks of Jervaulx) gathers something of the wildness of Mallerstang, perhaps recalling an ancestry in Hell Gill. Its actual source is unpretentious, with none of the travail Hugh Seat gives to the becks that become the Eden, and it bears its name from its first springing at Ure Head. Across it, the old road runs along the fellside by Shaws and High Dike, once an inn reputedly frequented by the highwayman 'Swift Nicks' Nevison, whose grey horse is said to have taken the gorge at Hell Gill Bridge in its stride. This track, perhaps once a Roman road, was much used by the end of the eighteenth century, when dalesfolk came from as far off as Ravenstonedale to sell refreshments to travellers, who included drovers with their herds, farmers and packmen. Nobility, too, used the road; no doubt the Lady Anne Clifford admired the view of Wild Boar Fell from here, though Mary, Queen of Scots, under restraint and bound for Bolton Castle in 1658, would be less likely to.

Near Shaw Paddock, formerly an inn known as The Bull, road and railway climb together towards Aisgill before their gentle descent of Mallerstang. If Wild Boar Fell dominates on the one hand, Mallerstang Edge is scarcely less impressive on the other. Southwards, the view along the Ure is almost as wild, with the spurs of Widdale Fell and Cotter End turning the gaze eastward into Wensleydale. At Lunds a rough road and dark avenue of conifers leads across the river to Place Farm and the youth hostel. A porchless, barnlike building, with a bell-turret – the rudest exterior imaginable – is Lunds church, dating probably from the first years of the eighteenth century. It stands in a large field where in summer cattle, goats and sheep graze together among lichened gravestones. In 1839

William Howitt found the building in a deplorable condition, with a hole in the roof, a broken bell, a bush for the door, and an enterprising warden who, in the absence of a bell, summoned worshippers vocally. Equally enterprising were the two musicians who in the tiny church performed the accompaniment to a performance of the Messiah – on trombone and clarinet! One dull December day when snow lay thickly in a cornice on Wild Boar Fell and icicles had silenced the waterfall of Hell Gill, I opened the door of Lunds church to find the room invitingly warm, and with electric lights and radiators burning in readiness for a service. Functionally furnished, the interior contained pews, font, reading desk, and a small organ and vestry; a text on the wall read "God is love". As I left I was aware of the wire and poles that in bringing electricity to the dale, and to this frozen hillside at 1,100 feet above sea level, achieved a miracle more impressive by far than in all the neon and tinsel of the city centre.

The Moorcock Inn stands in a hollow at the head of three dales – Garsdale, Mallerstang, and Wensleydale. After suffering mixed fortunes, the inn has now reopened and sheep dog trials there in June are well patronized. Eastward, the former Richmond turnpike rolls into Wensleydale, and the Yore picks up its first tributaries from side dales. Their number and names will tax the memory. Some may be passed by unnoticed despite their size. Mossdale, a small wooded gill where Turner painted, is obvious; Fossdale, where once the monks of Jervaulx had a grange, cuts back into Great Shunner Fell below Abbotside, which, as its name indicates, was monastic property. The road to Cotterdale is easily overlooked. It leads into a surprisingly green and spacious hollow watered by East and West Gills, and overlooked by the conifers of Nattles and Cotterdale plantations. I came to the village – 'Cotterdale Town' – in July, after an absence of some years. Gates had been replaced by cattle grids, and there were caravans by the river; evidently the dalesfolk who remain here are not so 'suspicious of strangers' as Ella Pontefract found forty years ago. Certainly its present inhabitants are more varied than the three families – the Halls, Kirks, and Kings – who used to live there, and who were perpetuated in the old rhyme:

> Three halls, two kirks, and a king,
> Same road out as goes in.

There is still only one road, which was being resurfaced on the day of my visit. It ends in a cluster of houses among trees, at its end passing narrowly and somewhat gloomily between Cotterdale Farm and Brunskill's Cottage. Stonecrop and swallows are the order of the day. So too are television aerials, garden tents, and windows of the Pilkington–Georgian period. The Methodist chapel, derelict on my last visit, has blossomed into a house of clean new stone, and before it in a grassed enclosure, formerly the burial ground, a few headstones are propped against the outer wall. There used to be a nameless gravestone which bore the words "We repose in peace here"; clearly this is no occasion on which to search for it. The coal pits on the moor above are forgotten; so too are the miners who sleep here at the end of the road in Cotterdale Town.

At the mouth of the dale the finest of a series of waterfalls is seen in the wooded limestone gorge of Cotter Force, perhaps best visited in winter when partly frozen, and when flocks of fieldfares frequent the beckside for its rowan and hawthorn berries; in spring, primrose and saxifrage grow profusely on the walls of the gorge. At either season, the cascade, concealed by foliage in summer, is seen to best effect among the clear light tracery of ash trees.

A mile down-dale, Appersett – 'the shieling near the apple tree' – is one of several villages whose name bears the Norse '-saetr' suffix. Its setting by a graceful bridge across the beck must have been idyllic two centuries ago. A broad green extending to the river bank; grey houses; the sound of water escaping from Widdale to more leisurely parent river, with cattle drinking – all the ingredients to inspire a Girtin or a Cotman. Regrettably, one has to be content with less than perfection, with an Appersett that, like so many other villages, has clearly had to come to terms with its roadside position in a busy through dale. There is a perpetual hint of the makeshift in its overgrown green hung with washing; a note of untidiness in the clutter of heavy vehicles; an air of the inappropriate in the undoubtedly functional alterations to its buildings. Transports and tractor parts wait around. Somewhere, there are animals. A man in an overall walks slowly along by the guest-house, a notice-board under his arm – 'Sorry, No Vacancies'. The internal combustion engine has much to answer for in the dales; dereliction to some, prosperity to others. It certainly brings the crowds, as did waggonettes a century ago, to Hardraw Scar across the river, where in a rocky amphitheatre behind The Green Dragon Inn water falls some ninety feet over a limestone step, and where, after a lapse of many years, brass bands again take advantage of favourable acoustics and hold an annual contest. The first competitions were held about 1885, and names like Black Dyke and Besses o' th' Barn are associated with them. On one occasion the famous equilibrist Blondin made an omelette on a tight-rope stretched across the gorge.

In a strategic position near the head of the dale, the market town of Hawes, less ancient than its neighbours Sedbusk, Burtersett and Gayle, serves as a staging post along the many routes that come to it from Ripon, Kendal, Ribblesdale, Wharfedale and Swaledale – the last two, by the high passes of Fleet Moss and Buttertubs respectively. Older folk call it 't'Haas, probably derived from the Anglo-Saxon 'haus', a mountain pass. Comparatively young by dales standards, Hawes has little to show in the way of antiquity; indeed, historical references do not go back beyond the fifteenth century. Among the few seventeenth-century houses is the old Quaker Rest House in the main street; now a temperance hotel, it bears the inscription 'Ano Dom 1668. God being with us who can be against. A.T.F.' In 1700 Hawes was granted a market charter, subsequently taking precedence over Askrigg. The coming of the Lancaster turnpike in 1795, and of the railway from Leyburn in 1879, later linking with the Settle-Carlisle line at Garsdale, further increased its importance. In 1959 and 1964 the lines up- and down-dale were closed, and the track eventually removed, but the station buildings have remained, a monument to the era of the North Eastern Railway and to the days when Victorian sightseers crowded its platforms, or transferred to waggonettes in the yard. From Wensleydale a nightly milk train left for London, and the sheds at Hawes echoed with the sound of hammer and chisel on quarry stone, and with the voices of livestock. In 1878 Mr Robinson, the Station Master, received £80 a year and was provided with a house. His assistant porter was a man called Little, whose wages matched his name; for 10 shillings a week he was expected to clean out cattle pens, in addition to his platform duties! After the link up with Garsdale, staff were responsible to the Midland Railway Company.

For over half a century the railway served Hawes, and the little red machine, still preserved, dispensed platform tickets. Today, Platform One is a botanist's paradise, and children – without ticket – fish in the beck at the end of Platform Two; but in the station buildings, now a National Park Information Centre, there is an air of prosperity. The high gables bristle, resplendent in new slates and paintwork; repairs and modifications go forward on every hand. On a summer day the yard is crowded with cars, and tourists inspect the station precincts and its displays; soon a folk museum in a refurbished goods-shed will be an added attraction. Not far away, the rope-maker's shop (under new management) is packed, and if it is Tuesday, one can visit the market hall and stalls in the main street, and buy anything from a carpet to a camellia. Long-distance coaches edge their way through the throng; campers from nearby caravan sites invade the shops; Landrovers and Lagondas jockey for position outside The Crown Hotel in an orgy of noise, colour and excitement that may well rival, or even surpass, that of the traditional fairs and markets of yester-year, now revered. One cannot help but regret the pass-ing of the old feasts and festivals, but in an understandable euphoria for the past it is as well to realize that human nature remains the same; only the scenario changes. We are told that Hawes Fair was bedevilled by petty thieves, and in 1798 two highwaymen were arrested there and taken to Bainbridge. One can understand the story of the dalesman who on such oc-casions always carried his money in his boots.

Undoubtedly the greatest single contribution to the economy of Hawes – and, indeed, of the dale – is the buying and selling of livestock. "Ya mun go t' th' Haas Mart fer't ram sales," a dalesman friend advised me. "Tek a few thousand, an ya'll git fit up!" He was quite serious. The sums of money that change hands are quite staggering. Any farmer hiding money in his boots today would need to wear wellingtons to such a sale. In 1972 livestock to the value of over £1,700,000 passed through the auction mart, including 11,000 cattle and 104,000 sheep. It is hardly surprising that the sales each Tuesday attract visitors, especially in summer, when crowds gather along the Bainbridge road, soon snarled with traffic; the motorist in a hurry would do well to use the Hardraw–Askrigg road on the north side of the river. By the sheds, 'General Supplies' from Kirkby Stephen stands next to 'Wholesale Veterinary Products' from Kendal. An Askrigg cattle truck manoeuvres around another bearing the renowned name of 'Guy' from Muker. Holidaymakers rub shoulders with farmers, and shepherds with academics. A school-teacher directs a project at a cattle pen draped with ten-year-olds. In the main sale room, ringed with raked seats but still empty, there is the air of a Roman circus, with games about to begin. Or is it a bullfight? An *aficionado* with a mop and a tin of green paint enters the amphitheatre and makes a few final adjustments. Clean sawdust is spread on the floor. It is 10.30 a.m., and in answer to my enquiry about the starting time, the man replies, "In about ten minutes wi' a few fat sheep." I make the necessary conversion from D. T. (Dalesman's Time) to B.S.T. Promptly at 11 a.m., at the ringing of a bell, a sliding door opens and the white-coated Emperor and his attendants take their place on the rostrum. A rush of sheep to the scales, some hieroglyphics on a slate, a dab of green on each animal, and the contest has begun. There is a burst of acoustic mumbo-jumbo, no doubt to propitiate some pagan diety: "20. 18, 20. 19 . . ." A cryptic response from the faithful elicits "21. 40, 21. 50 . . ." The smell of beasts, and men, from the arena. "22. 30, 22. 40 . . ." The sound of the gavel descending, and of the clipping of ears. A burst of activity from the gladiator with the green paint, who replaces soiled sawdust, and who is now reduced to open waistcoat and dangling watch-chain; the battered trilby is a fixture. Outside in the refreshment room the air is lethal with pipe smoke, and the talk is of beasts and men. This is no place for a townsman – even a Yorkshire one. On the road a white caravan and a cattle truck have reached an impasse, halting traffic. The escape to the hayfields is open, and one can recover beneath the pink briar roses, and dream of another Hawes. That, perhaps, of the quiet days that follow Christmas, when one can follow the flagged field path, white with frost, towards the river, and listen to the pleasantly diminished sound of 'Jesus shall reign' from Hawes band outside the youth hostel.

There are a number of these flagged paths around Hawes; one long one connects the village with Burtersett. One man who knows more than most about them is seventy-five-years-old Kit Calvert, M.B.E., whose services to the Dales are renowned. He recalls that many of them were the result of a feud between farmers and quarrymen, who used to walk, sometimes in groups, to and from work across the fields. In so doing, much valuable grass was lost, and to prevent this, the quarry provided flags and the farmer had them laid "all't way ta Bootasitt". A legal ruling demanded a minimum width of three feet, but human nature being what it is, the venture on the whole proved abortive, and the feud continued.

From Dodd Fell the Duerley Beck flows down Sleddale to the Yore, and with a flourish of exhibitionism divides the village of Gayle, a settlement of Celtic origin. It is all river – ford, and bridge and waterfall – and people and houses must take pot luck. From Greensett the road twists indecisively at the bridge, and forks. One arm emerges unscathed, and runs down past the cheese factory to Hawes. Another finds the back way out towards Bainbridge. What is left goes to earth into a number of narrow alleyways, or 'wynds', among houses that back on to the hill. One building at least has made the most of the beck – Gayle Mill, which after the 1780s was concerned with cotton, flax, and wool spinning, though latterly it survived as a sawmill.

What has been said of knitting in Dentdale may also be said of Wensleydale; what Dent Town was to the former, Gayle was to the latter. Men, women, and children knitted, first from wool spun in the home, and later from machine-spun yarn. Mills took the place of travelling hosiers. At Hawes, up to twenty people were employed in the mill, which supplied four hundred hand knitters in the area. By the end of the nineteenth entury, hand knitting had almost ceased.

One daleswoman who lived close to Gayle Mill for most of her life was Betty Allen, who, over a cup of tea and a piece of her home-made Gayle 'bannock', often recalled her early days in the village. As a girl she had helped her mother to knit 'waders' (stockings). Her job was to make the tops – "purl and plain, ye know". They were taken down to Hawes, where Dover's carrier from Sedbergh used to park his horse and waggon in front of The Crown Hotel. Mother used to produce four to six stockings a week, besides doing her day's work, and walking over Fleet Moss to Oughtershaw, in Wharfedale, regularly, to visit her aged parents. "At night she would knit for all she was worth, puir thing! Wi've known hard times, I might tell you!"

Betty's memories of cheese-making went back to her granny's house, which always had "a piece of kezzup" hung in the window. Keslop, the dried stomach of a calf, was used instead of rennet, to separate curds and whey. Betty remembered the "big copper kettle", and removing the whey, which was good to drink. The curds were kneaded; her job included "shakin' and breakin' it up with a trellis-wire with a handle" (a breaker). Then came the wooden cheese press, and the mopping up; drying and bandaging; and the large earthenware pots in which the cheeses were 'cured' in brine. "Wi put water in a big pan on the fire, and put in salt till an egg would float." Not the least laborious job was to clean the utensils afterwards in the beck – "Wi scrubbed it wi' sand on a bink till it was spotless!" The beck still makes its music, but Betty can no longer hear it.

"It's a luv'ly little village is Gayle. Thi're all so friendly, I don't go away on holiday," Betty told me, the last time I saw her. "Ther's seventy-two or three houses, and folk keeps coming, and dying. Ah count 'em when ah can't sleep." One hopes that the name of Betty Allen is still remembered by some other wakeful veteran of the dale.

In the upper part of Wensleydale spoil heaps on the hillside bear witness to past exploitation of the sandstones of the Yoredale series. Stone for houses and barns, walling stones, and flags for roofing were taken from the hillsides, often from underground workings. One comes across them at Hardraw, and on Stags Fell. Each bed had a characteristic colour, or texture. Stags Fell was hard, and that from Sedbusk, light in colour. In Burtersett, older folk remember the heyday of their own quarries, which closed in 1929. Above the village are the derelict remains of dressing sheds and levels driven deep into the hillside. "Ye can still git in ta Metcalfe's quarries," one old lady told me, " – but ye'd better not!" Every level and its 'off-shots' had a name: Red Gate, Savey, Fancy End, and Peacock. Ponies brought out large slabs up to six inches thick on a tramway, and the stone was rough dressed in a shed at the mouth of the tunnel. "It wer good to work – beat all't bricks". Village folk remembered the stables, and horses, and waggons with a 'slipper' on a chain, and the struggle down the hill to Hawes Station four times a day. There the stone was again dressed before leaving by train, perhaps for the growing towns of Lancashire. At the height of their activity, the quarries employed over a hundred men, some of whom walked over from Sedbusk or Gayle with their food in a tin box or a cloth. 'Blow-up time' was at 7.30 a.m., and 'Billy Willie' at the village shop opened early for half an hour to sell tobacco to the quarry workers. He kept two boxes for 'twist', one with halfpenny 'screws' and the other with penny. In addition to dressing sheds, there were wooden cranes, stables, and a black-smith's shop where horses were shod and tools sharpened.

I spoke to Ernest Brown, tidying up on the patch of grass that marks the centre of the hamlet. As a lad, he used to ride back from school in Hawes on weekdays on the empty quarry carts, and on Sunday he attended worship twice: at church in the morning, and round the corner in the chapel in the afternoon. There used to be three shops in the village; one a butcher's, with a 'hung-house' (slaughterhouse). He recalled the cottages built for quarry workers, who on Sundays used to work up a thirst by walking over to Countersett, slaking it with ale from the back door of The Boar Inn.

The inn has long disappeared, as have many of the dalesfolk of Burtersett – the Ivesons, Walkers, and Dinsdales. Kit Calvert, a native of 'Bootasitt', will give you a history of Wensleydale names, of the Metcalfes and the Rouths, and recalls the 'good old days' in the village. His grandmother Mary, who knitted without even looking down, prepared meals with a half-made stocking on its needles dangling from her sheath. Farmers helped each other, especially at haytime, and wives gathered to help prepare a special meal – the 'mell supper'. "Wi'd boiled ham, and two gallon o' beer, and ginger pop for us kiddies," recounts Kit, "wi'd a right good tuck-in!" Then music followed; fiddle, concertina or American organ. "Them as could sang, and them as couldn't used to try." In a long room above the quarry stables young folk danced, and 't'owd 'uns' played nap or 'Fox and Geese'. Bonfire night was a memorable occasion, when a procession marched around the village, led by Guy Fawkes on a chair. Before the days of 'dipping', sheep were salved with a mixture of "Stockholm Tar and rancid Russian butter", which came in barrels. These the village lads acquired when empty, to be set alight and used in the bonfire procession. "Finest sight I ever saw were twenty-six barrels, an' fat, an' paraffin; wi lit 'em, and carried 'em down

Lowgate and round East Lane past mi grandmother's."

In the village now there are some sixty or eighty locals left, but not as many children as there used to be. Many of the present inhabitants are off-comers. Perhaps the Norse who first settled here beneath Wether Fell, in the 'shieling by the alders', were once regarded in the same light by the Britons next door in Gayle. I jokingly suggested that soon Burtersett would be on the short list for the Best Kept Village title. Ernest rested on his scythe and delivered a parting shot. "Beautiful - nay! Too many farmers; too much muck!" Dalesfolk are nothing if not forthright, even at seventy!

XII

THE DALE OF MANY DELIGHTS

THOSE WHO PASS from Burtersett to the Roman road and Semerdale will miss the charming views of the dale presented from the lower hillside, where a field path leads over towards Bainbridge. Of course, one must be prepared at the risk of grazed knees to squeeze through 'stee holes' in the walls, to negotiate nettle beds, and to pass over wobbling slabs of Burtersett flags set across the many watercourses. In July, the walk can be very rewarding. Masses of meadowsweet fill damp hollows where streamlets lose their force. Trees, clustering around outbarns, provide shelter from sun and wind, and are frequented by spotted flycatchers. Every croft and barnyard has its pied wagtails, and steep grassy banks and odd corners where the machine cannot get are gay with betony, hawkbits, hare-bell, knapweed and tormentil, which attract butterflies, espec-ially meadow brown and small heath. Thistles are fast ripening, and attract goldfinches in family parties, or 'charms'; even into August the young are still being fed on wall tops, the province also of wheatears, white-rumped and restless. If one excepts swallow and martin, which are still breeding, birds generally are self-effacing and silent at this time of the year.

There are two sorts of pleasure for those who walk the by-ways of the dales: the expected, and the unexpected. The first are awaited with anticipation – a bird, a view, a flower – each in its season, and the year would be incomplete without them. The second come as a pleasant surprise – a bonus in an already beneficient landscape. Into this category I would put the tiny mill which, despite its advanced years, still stands to attention behind an elm and an elderberry within sight of Burtersett. Its 'eyes' are blind, and the floors of its three storeys are gone, but the jackdaws in the roof are contented enough. Once a silk mill, it is remembered by folks in the village as 't'Condle Mill', where tallow candles were made for domestic use, and to light the darkness of the subterranean quarries above. A number of pieces of tow were fastened to a wheel and

143

lowered through a hole in the floor into the beck to harden. Primitive as the process was, some skill was required to produce candles of uniform thickness, and the work of 'Billy Tommy Willie' Metcalfe was in great demand. "Condle Willie's were good," an old man told me, "but chap as followed 'im med pear-shaped condles!" The coming of wax candles and lamps put an end to the activities of the mill and Willie's successor.

Some of the effects of the Ice Age are visible along the upper part of the dale where drumlins were left behind by the retreating Wensleydale glacier; they are clearly seen as rounded hillocks at Lady Hill and near Bainbridge. In side-dales, too, moraines of glacial debris were left, and lakes impounded. Most of these disappeared, as valleys silted up with level areas of alluvium, which appear now as fertile meadowland.

One lake which remains is Semerwater, on whose shores pile dwellings and artifacts of Bronze and Iron Age man were found when the level was lowered in 1937. Becks from Cragdale, Raydale and Bardale unite to feed the lake, which is drained by the swift River Bain. This river, reputedly the shortest in England, cuts its way down through glacial deposits, and with considerable turbulence passes through Bainbridge to the Yore. The fame of Semerwater has spread beyond the dale; in northern schoolrooms the legend of the sunken city, doomed for its lack of charity, is remembered in one of the many versions of the story:

> Once there stood by Semerwater
> A mickle town and tall,
> King's tower, and Queen's bower,
> And the wakeman on the wall

Today the wakeman must be a very worried man. From April to October yachts and power boats disturb his perambulations. In autumn, quiet returns, and whooper swans gather on the unruffled waters of the lake. Whichever way one comes by road to Semerdale, the first reaction may well be of surprise – that one has suddenly been transported to Lakeland. On closer observation there are, of course, differences. At Semerwater the hills are less demonstrative, and roll down to the water's edge; their decor, too, is Pennine, and therefore restrained. Outcrops are manifestly limestone, and if one excepts the wall of Addle-brough, undramatic. Yet the setting is perfect. Three valleys unite on the level floor of the dale – 'Cragd'le', 'Rayd'le', and 'Bard'le'. Say that quickly and you have the sound of boots on the stony track that leads by Cragdale over the Stake to Buckden. Raydale, with mature and young woodland on its slopes, loses itself in Fleet Moss. Bardale is long and straight, as befits a dale that once echoed to the sound of Roman legionaries on the march from Virosidum. At its foot Marsett, one of a trio of hamlets that keep watch on Semerwater, is scarcely tidy, and certainly not for the tourist. One always gets the impression that only work goes on there! Close by, Stalling Busk is a delight, benefiting from a more elevated site. There are superb views. The little church of St Matthew, sharp buttressed, has a most unusual exterior, as though the original plan had got lost altogether. The ruin of the old church lower down the hill offers a fine excuse for a walk through the fields, passing through the hamlet. One cottage has a row of large milk kits, beautifully rusty, as a boundary; at another, an old 'slopstone' lies discarded in the garden. Stone flags, probably from Burtersett quarries, are on view everywhere. On my last visit, one house was having a new roof of old flags!

Closer to civilization, Countersett lies in a hollow on the hillside overlooking the lake. Behind the Hall, where George Fox stayed in 1677, is the Friends' Meeting House, dated 1710; here according to the notice-board, meetings for worship can be held 'by arrangement'. Personally I can never think of Countersett without applauding Mrs Fawcett's choice of table covers (or were they curtains?). Mary – "my husband's a Swaledale Fawcett" – lives next door to the meeting house, which I had paused to look at. It was one of those greyer-than-grey days which can only happen in the north country – grey hills, grey road, grey houses, and, to borrow from Hilaire Belloc, skies that were also "fast and grey". Every shepherd knows such conditions which often linger for days at the end of summer. Even the enthusiast finds them depressing; I certainly did, as I leaned over the gate at Mary Fawcett's. Then I saw the covers, a whole lineful hanging out to dry. Bright and red and cheerful, against the omniscient grey. I spoke to Mary who used to farm in the days when the village had five farms. Now it has one, and a fair number of renovated cottages. I asked her about Semerwater, and the city which folk have reputedly glimpsed below the surface. "Ah've lived 'ere twenty-six years," she assured me, "and ah've nivver sin nowt!"

From Semerdale, the River Bain enters Bainbridge with a flourish of falling water, a fitting introduction to one of the most spacious and pleasant villages in the dales. The breadth of the green is nicely broken by trees, and the view bounded by the white façade of The Rose and Crown, which pleasingly separates village from more distant fells. By the ancient stocks a small notice-board bears a historical sketch of the village from about A.D. 80, when the Romans built the first of their forts on Brough Hill, a green mound of glacial debris overlooking the village. A road connected with Aldborough (Isurium), near Boroughbridge, and another to the south-west passed over Wether and Cam Fells to link with the Lune valley and with Ribchester, on the Ribble. A southern route flanks Addlebrough and passes by Stalling Busk to Kidstones and Wharfedale. Between Holyrood and Shrove Tide, i.e. in autumn and winter, it has long been the custom to sound the Forest Horn each evening, a practice said to date back to Norman times, and intended to guide travellers to the safety of "the towne of Beynbrigge". For many years this has been done by members of the Metcalfe family. Across the way, in The Rose and Crown, a fifteenth-century hostelry, one can see the present horn, which hangs in the entrance hall alongside some preserved specimens of trout taken locally. The Ure is also known for its grayling, barbel and crayfish, and in 1968 salmon parr were introduced experimentally; bream occur in Semerwater.

It is clear that the good folk of Bainbridge take a pride in their village. Under the trees crocuses and snowdrops add a welcome note of colour at the end of winter. Perhaps the finest display is in early May, when masses of jonquils and daffodils bloom on the south side of the green.

Across the Yore, a stile by the bridge gives access to the river bank, and by way of a flagged path, to Hocket Bridge, a tiny pack-horse bridge spanning Grange Beck. This stream and the River Bain enter the Yore together along a reach where the parent stream, brown and beautiful, moves slowly beneath a canopy of foliage. In August, bellflower, marjoram, and rest harrow line its banks. Close at hand a picturesque cottage hung with rambler roses stands on the site of the chantry chapel of Fors Abbey, a Cistercian house established hereabouts in 1145.

The land proved unworkable and the climate inclement, and the place was abandoned after eleven years in favour of Jervaulx, beyond the limits of the forest. Nearby Coleby Hall, a manor house dating from 1633, may well contain some of the stone from the abbey. Just off the Askrigg road, a little way up Grange Beck, an ancient bridge with ribbed arches lies almost hidden among trees, its walls vaulted across a horizontal base of natural limestone. From it, a field path leads into the wooded amphitheatre of Abbey Fors ('Force'), a miniature Hardraw, where the waters of the beck fall some thirty feet into a wagtail-haunted pool.

Beyond the almshouses endowed by Christopher Alderson in 1807, at the approaches to Askrigg, two major streams, Sargill and Cogill Becks which rise on Muker and Oxnop Commons, join the Yore, the latter as Paddock Beck, where three mills once operated in close proximity. Low Mill has gone; the old flax mill is now converted; and the upper, or West Mill, which was a corn mill and which is now empty, pending restoration. Here the mill wheel, perhaps fourteen feet in diameter, can still be seen, as can the stone piers of the mill race, which terminates in a metal trough, overshooting the wheel. A field path leading upstream gives excellent views of the village, while southward the prospect of Addlebrough top, its lower scarps, and a conspicuous elongated drumlin on the valley floor, is a composition of aesthetically pleasing horizontals.

Few visitors will want to miss Mill Gill Force, clamorous in a wooded ravine that reminds one of the deep cloughs of Todmorden and Hebden Bridge. All the ingredients are here – falls, rocks, and mills lost among deep woodland. At Mill Gill, however, a more luxuriant growth indicates the presence of limestone. The path is steep and wet, ending on a boulder-littered floor beneath a considerable cascade pouring from a notch in the limestone sill. The impression in summer from the foot of the fall is one of claustrophobia – a surfeit of sound in a green twilight. Nowhere, not even at Hardraw, do the Yoredales express themselves more effectively than above the attenuated bellflowers and enchanter's nightshade that strain for the light in Mill Gill.

On the steep slope the etiolated stems of bluebell and dog's mercury lie in rows, heads downwards, flattened by drainage after every shower. It is a relief to escape to the light of summer, and to the whimsical signpost that points the way across the fields to a destination which has been missed by even that most delightful historian of the dales, the peerless Miss Pontefract; it is called 'Single File'!

Few places have been so fully documented as Askrigg, the 'Ascric' (Ash-ridge?) of Domesday Book. To attempt to embellish it or amplify these accounts would be an impertinence to the indefatigable scholarship of the Misses Hartley and Ingilby. Simply, its story is one of former importance, and of a decline from the end of the eighteenth century when the new turnpike road brought favour to Hawes. Askrigg's market charter dates from 1587, and the village became a centre for textiles, brewing, lead, and clock-making. Like them, the Old Hall that overlooked the bull ring and stepped market cross is gone, gutted by fire in 1935, and the dale is poorer for its loss. On the west side of the square, the church of St Oswald dates from the thirteenth to the sixteenth centuries, with later restoration. A broad-flagged path traverses the churchyard to outlying cottages, and gives access to the south door. One hot summer morning during the Flower Festival I came to St Oswald's. In the porch an overcrowded swallow's nest brimful with fledglings threatened every moment to jettison its occupants. Inside the church, a remarkable ribbed roof echoed with the twittering of another swallow which had entered by the clerestory windows; it was as if the August countryside had come indoors. There was the scent of flowers everywhere; petals on the floor; bright doves in silk on the altar; and above the door a large clock face, without hands, refused to record the passing of the summer days. On it, the inscription "Deface me not. I mean no ill. I stand to serve. You for good will."

Outside in the sun, swifts scream above the village street, which climbs and bends by tall houses and, apparently, towards better things. Another bend, and town-houses suddenly give way to cottages. One is left with a feeling of disappointment for a town that one expects, but which never materializes. The King's Arms (c. "1750 – Ye Olde Coaching Hostelry") capitulates to The Crown Inn (Cameron's Ales) and to the older part of the village. Yet, viewed from Mill Gill or from Cubeck, the prospect of Askrigg cannot be faulted. One of the most pleasing of sights is that above its roof-tops as one climbs from the village on the road to Swaledale, a route remarkable for its scenic appeal. A mile or so above Askrigg, beyond the track that leads to Whitfield Gill, the elevated valley of Semerdale rises across the valley, its lake too veiled and distant to sparkle, too much against the light to be colourful. By it, flat topped and equally veiled, Addlebrough sits squarely with Penhill at the gates of Bishopdale. Oxnop, with its spectacular limestone scarp, its pavement, and heather moors, lead on to Summer Lodge Tarn, The Fleak, and to the views of West Bolton Moor and the derelict mining ground of Beldon. In this monochrome of high moors the flowering of heather and the coming of snow are the only perceptible indications of the changing year.

From Askrigg, it is a short journey to Aysgarth. Lesser roads on each side of the valley follow the line of limestone scarp, level and direct, with enchanting views across the dale. The Yore can be crossed near Worton, and there is a succession of hamlets and villages: Woodhall, Cubeck, and the delightful Thornton Rust, with its old-world cottages, many with outside stairs. On the north side of the river, with its back to the lowest step of scarp, and overhung by trees, is Nappa Hall, the ancestral home until 1756 of the Metcalfe family. Now a farmhouse, it dates from the mid-fifteenth century, with later additions. A central hall overlooking a courtyard lies between two cross wings, the west one in the form of a castellated pele tower. The Metcalfes, who came into the dale in the twelfth century, were a most notable, influential, and prolific family. Among the offices they held were those of Master Forester, and High Sheriff of Yorkshire. It is said that Sir Christopher in 1556 led three hundred of the Metcalfe clan, mounted on white horses, when he attended the judges at York. One wonders if the pages of a telephone directory might offer a modern and equally revealing parallel.

Beyond the hidden hamlet of Woodall and Woodall Park, once a royal hunting ground, the rounded eminence of Lady Hill with its sentinel pines dominates the dale bottom. To ensure succession, new trees have been planted here by the National Park Authority. Woodland, mainly ash, covers the lower scarp of Ivy Scar, running round to Ballowfield, remarkable for its variety of wild flowers. By a damp stretch of streamside in August I counted over twenty species, including dropwort, thrift, grass of Parnassus, and scabious. Unfortunately, this productive ground is increasingly threatened in summer by the inconsiderate pitching of tents, and by over-night caravans. East of Ballowfield, the quiescent Yore undergoes a change of character, spilling in lively fashion over steps of limestone in three sets of impressive falls which are infinitely better known that the village itself, and to which thousands of tourists have come by road and rail. In 1772 Thomas Pennant was greatly impressed: "The scenery . . . is most commonly picturesque. The banks on both sides are lofty, rocky, and darkened with trees. Above the bridge, two ir-regular precipices cross the river, down which the water falls in beautiful cascades which are seen to great advantage from below." Leland found the falls awe-inspiring. Ruskin knew them, and Turner painted them. The idea of a brick viaduct across the valley hereabouts, and a railway line to link with Kettlewell via Bishopdale, would seem unthinkable, yet in 1880 such a proposal was the cause for the formation of a Defence Association supported by many prominent names. The scheme fell through, and eventually even the Wensleydale line was closed and removed. Today, in summer, cars and coaches pack extended parking grounds, and visitors have the added attraction of a refreshment room and an information centre. They can follow a nature trail, walk in woodland, or scramble down slippery banks to view the cascades, truly magnificent after rain. Across the Upper Falls there are the remains of a mill race which supplied water to Yore Mill, now a carriage museum. Corn, cotton and wool have all played their part in the story of the mill, which was destroyed by fire and rebuilt in 1853. Like the mill at Hawes, Yore Mill had a contract for the supply of red shirts for Garibaldi's Italian army. The road bridge, once a narrow pack-horse bridge, was built at the bequest of James Sedgwick in 1594, but has since been modified to cope with increasing traffic.

Aysgarth, of Norse origin ('a clearing among oaks'), has historical associations, though the present village, situated on a coaching route and reflecting the coming of the railway, is fairly modern. At Castle Dykes, south of the river, a mound and ditch probably originated in the Bronze Age. St Andrew's, once the church of the Forest of Wensleydale, dated from Norman times, but was largely rebuilt in 1866. It has pews with poppy heads of the Ripon school of carvers dated about 1506, a reading desk and a fine rood screen, perhaps brought here from Jervaulx Abbey. The ancient parish of Aysgarth, covering almost 82,000 acres and the largest in England, once extended to Lunds, at the head of Mallerstang.

In Wensleydale there is a breadth and freedom which no other dale can equal. Yet it is often the side-valleys, especially the 'blind' ones, that captivate with their intimacy. The road climbs into them, often by way of gate or cattle grid; twists over moraine or spur; passes a last lonely farmstead; and as a track peters out in the high pastures. Or perhaps the way up-dale ends as a sled track, disappearing among bracken, or finally lost among peat hags. Frequently the names of these dales are as wildly primitive as their appearance; how many are there, one wonders, that assume the anonymity of such descriptions as 'Langdale', 'Grizedale', or 'Sleddale'? Look to the rear, as it were, of the 'giants', and you will find them; behind Whernside, Penyghent, or Great Shunner, where one can tramp all day, and seldom see another human.

Walden has this air of seclusion, with a beck that rises at 2,000 feet in the fastnesses of Buckden Pike. There are remains of coal pits, and lead mines at Walden Head and Dovescar, though on a minor scale. In the gill near Cote Farm a small smelt mill flourished in the early eighteenth century, and by it a track leads over the saddle between Penhill and Harlow Hill (1,758 feet). Two or three lonely houses lie at the end of the road at Walden Head, and on the east side of the valley, a similar road leads to White Row, which looks across to Wasset Fell (1,610 feet) flanked by conifer plantations. The way to Walden passes through West Burton, a delightful village which exhausts superlatives. The spacious green has a tapered cross with steps - a spire once crowned with a weather-cock which on Feast Day used to be decorated with ribbons and carried round the houses. This emblem now surmounts the roof of a large converted barn nearby. The Fox and Hounds is embellished with a romantic picture of the hunt resting above the Yore, and looks across the green with its inevitable horses, also resting. At 5 o'clock on a summer afternoon a herd of cows straggles unhurriedly past the Methodist chapel to the end of the village; a pony dozes. Nothing here ever hurries, it seems. School has not yet reopened, and at the bottom end of the green, opposite 'Galloway House, 1656', the Aussies are being outplayed in the Burton version of the Fourth Test. Evidently there is one vital connection with the outside world. It is a pity, in one sense, that there is so much in the village to claim the attention, for in one's eagerness to see its attractions one may miss the waterfalls, dismissed so perfunctorily in some guide-books. Cauldron Falls lie at the north-eastern end of the village, where Walden Beck cuts its way through a wooded gorge to form a limestone amphitheatre of unexpected width. A large pool lies beneath a ponderous undercut of rock; being open, the place lacks the oppressiveness of, say, Mill Gill Force at Askrigg. An ancient stone bridge with low parapets, almost submerged in sycamores, looks across to a former mill race, where the remains of a sluice gate are still visible. One can trace its course down to the mill building, now converted to flats, which stands with cottages in this secluded corner below the village.

At Eshington Bridge, Bishopdale Beck passes down to join the Yore, with West Burton and Thoralby – 'Thorold's Farm'? – guarding the entrance to a side-dale almost blocked by moraine; indeed, from some viewpoints the entrances to Walden and Bishopdale become one. The two are separated by Naughtberry Hill (1,652 feet), but the latter dale, enclosed though it is, is less remote, as one would expect in a 'through' valley. Six miles up-dale from Thoralby the road climbs over Kidstones Pass to Wharfedale, and recent road widening, bringing visitors by coach on a 'Dales Circular', has not improved its seclusion. Despite this detraction, Bishopdale has much to offer scenically; the panorama it affords as one tops the pass from Buckden, or in its mounting views of limestone scarp, one upon the other, as one ascends to the dale head. Those who pass through in haste to the famous falls at Aysgarth will miss the lesser-known ones which are the hidden charms of Bishopdale – at Heaning Gill, near Thoralby ('on the sunny side'), and in the ravine of Foss Gill, in mid dale, where there is a whole series of cascades. Naughtberry Hill may be climbed from the hamlet of Newbiggin ('on the money side'), and there are upland paths to the plantations of Waldendale, and to West Burton. A little further down Walden Beck, by Flanders Hall, a pack-horse bridge carries the old road over the scar and by West Witton Moor to Middleham, passing above the obelisk known as Templar's Chapel, and the hamlet of Swinithwaite.

From the tumultuous reaches of Aysgarth the Yore sets a more placid course through the very heart of Wensleydale for Redmire and the woods of Bolton Hall. Villages stand above it on the lowest terraces of limestone, and their houses, bedecked with roses in August, look across the river to each other almost pensively, as if recalling their former glory. In the days when coal and lead were mined, the hills were far more than a scenic backdrop, and the market, feast days and fairs, important functions. At West Witton, the feast went on for three days. Today, in August, you may still see a notice announcing "West Witton Feast, Sports, and Cottage Show, Open Fell Race, and the Burning of Bartle". At this traditional ceremony an effigy is carried at dusk past The Fox and Hounds by two or three local lads, to a bonfire at the end of the village. Starting time is uncertain. "It depends how much false courage they need," one villager told me. As the procession progresses, one youth calls out the time-honoured words:

> At Pen Hill Crags he tore his rags;
> At Hunter's Thorn he blew his horn;
> At Capplebank Stee he broke his knee;
> At Grisgill beck he broke his neck;
> At Wadham's End he couldn't fend;
> At Grisgill End he made his end.

At Grass Gill 'Owd Bartle' is consigned to the flames.

At Redmire, in September, the feast lasted a week, and included sports. Carperby, the birthplace of the breed of sheep known as 'Wensleydales', lies below a hillside terraced with lynchets. It was a centre of Quakerism, and was visited by George Fox. On the green an old cross, in a setting unfortunately marred by a criss-cross of wires and poles, dates from 1674, though the market charter of the village was granted in 1303. Splendid walks by field paths lead down across the old railway line to Aysgarth Falls.

A celebrated landmark of the dales, best seen from across the valley, near Swinithwaite, where it is framed repeatedly along a fine avenue of trees, is Bolton Castle, a fortified manor house founded by Richard Scrope and built in the latter part of the fourteenth century; its licence to crenellate was granted in 1379. At its completion it represented complete security – four towers with living quarters surrounding a courtyard. Its chief function was residential, and it had a chapel, consecrated in 1399, and its own well, brew-house, and bake-house. In an apartment in the south-west tower, Mary, Queen of Scots was held prisoner from July 1568 until January 1569. There is a story of her attempted escape, in which she was assisted by one Kit Norton of Rylstone. According to tradition the lady was recaptured on Leyburn Shawl, and the name of 'Queen's Gap' still clings to a section of this wooded scarp. Those of a romantic turn of mind who visit the Shawl may be disappointed. The view is superb, but the presence of quarries nearby, where the hill is gradually being removed to the iron works of Teesside, is, to say the least, distracting.

The thirteenth Lord Scrope died in 1630, and the estate passed to his son-in-law Charles Powlett, who, having been created Duke of Bolton in 1689, built nearby Bolton Hall. Today visitors may see the remains of the castle, dine in its restaurant, and inspect its folk museum. The adjoining village, once dependent upon the castle, flourished during the lead-mining era, and consists simply of a row of cottages on each side of a village green.

At the end of the village, past the Methodist chapel, the road narrows. There are magnificent views of Penhill, and of the jaws of Waldendale. By an ancient ford and an overgrown track called 'Watery Lane', grassy ridges in a field near the river mark the site of the lost village of Thoresby. Towards the end of August there are already signs of the advancing year; a glow of nasturtiums from the last gardens of Castle Bolton, where an old man is "clearin' up a bit for t'back end". Against the walls the green and gold of sweet cicely, whose foliage brought the perfume of aniseed in spring, is a wonderful blend of colour, each yellowing clump crowned with a spot of black, like the dotting of a tall letter 'i'. Long banks of it are still standing high along the road past Apedale Beck, and by the way that leads to Redmire, and to the heights of Preston Moor. Here the chimney of Cobscar smelt-mill presides over a desolation of stones and heather knolls, with the remains of filled-in shafts and the circular mounds and hollows of bell pits. Coal and lead were mined hereabouts; coal on the moor above, where in the eighteenth and nineteenth centuries shafts were sunk into the millstone grit to a depth of a hundred feet; and lead at Cobscar, and below at Keld Head. The long flue

that extended from Gillfield Wood two miles away can still be
seen as a line of stones across the moor, its arched roof, once
sealed with turf, collapsed. There is the same air of silence and
solemnity about the ruined smelt-mill that one experiences at
Hurst and Old Gang in Swaledale, and across the way among
the hushings and rubble of Apedale. Half a mile away among
the spoil heaps, Calamine House still bears traces of croft walls
and the human presence. Keld Head was Wensleydale's largest
mine, employing in its heyday over three hundred men, whose
usual wage was two and sixpence (12½p) a day. In one year the
mine, which extended a mile into the hill and 160 fathoms
from top to bottom, produced 1,374 tons of smelted ore. Its
final closure was due to flooding and to the declining price of
lead. The smelt-mill chimney remains a memorial to the men
who dug, dressed, smelted and weighed, and to the lads who
cleaned the chimneys and pumped air to the levels. One accepts
it as part of the landscape, which is more than can be said of
the two modern masts on Ivy Scar. It is a part of the 'natural'
scene, a landmark to be looked for from miles away on Penhill
or Addlebrough. Perhaps the distinction can best be summed
up in the words of a dalesman from the Lancashire border,
who, holidaying in Wensleydale, was asked by his amazed wife
how Cobscar chimney came to be built. "Don't be daft," he
replied, "it's allus bin thur!"

The views from Preston Scar and Leyburn Shawl are scarcely
to be surpassed; from this angle against the light the atmos-
pheric qualities of the great hollow of the dale are accentuated.
The traveller who arrives from the south by way of Coverdale,
Carlton and Melmerby Moor, pausing beneath the scarp of
Penhill, will, on the other hand, be enthralled by colour. In late
August it is particularly impressive, not only for the purple
sweep of its grouse moors, but for the bracken slopes on the
eastern side of the hill. Lost among the green sea of growth that
hides sheep, rock, and ring ouzel alike, an old track, down
which stone and peat were once carted, descends the hillside
towards Carlton. A stone cairn marks the spot where Penhill's
beacons were fired, and on the west side at Nab End are the
remains of Celtic enclosures. Indeed the prefix of the name
'Penhill', meaning 'head' or 'hill', is British in derivation,
though many of the villages at its feet recall the Norse –
Arkleside, Carlton and Scrafton. The years fall lightly on these

broad wastes of the Pennines, and, resting among the heather, one's imagination rolls back the centuries. A pole, a wire, and a vapour trail in the sky, are all that separate past from present. Across these slopes where Mary, Queen of Scots, watched summer become winter and the Pilgrimage of Grace cast its shadow, the year reaches its brief zenith, dry and audible in the heather. The sound of guns on Scrafton Moor, shrouded and innocuous; the unseen grasshopper's urgent metronome; drifting thistledown, bound on August's trade winds to the ports of Swaledale, and beyond, ring the knell of passing summer on this sunlit island in the mist. From Penhill's sonorous bracken slopes it is a short step to Melmerby, past gathering swallows on the roofs of Agglethorpe, and to Wensley by the Yore.

A pleasanter place cannot be imagined than the village that gave its name to the dale. Its market charter dates from 1202, but in 1563 a plague "most hote and fearfull" resulted in an exodus of inhabitants; many of the less fortunate were buried away from the churchyard, on what is now Chapel Hill. Subsequently the village surrendered its importance to Askrigg. Across the way from The Three Horse Shoes inn, the trees beneath which John Wesley once preached, and the dalesfolk held their celebrations, are gone, though replacements have been planted. Iron gates close by give access to the parkland of Bolton Hall, built in 1678 by the Marquess of Winchester, the first Duke of Bolton; it was modified in 1902 after being damaged by fire, and is renowned for its collection of paintings.

In the parish church, one of the most impressive of dales churches, two large box pews were installed by the third duke, and bear hymn books inscribed with family names. Above the pews hangs the faded banner of the Loyal Dales Volunteers, mustered to resist Napoleon, and a large escutcheon bearing the Bolton and the Royal Arms. A wooden screen and reliquary, reputedly the only one of its kind in England, and which may have contained the remains of St Agatha, came from Easby Abbey. On the floor of the sanctuary some beautiful brasses commemorate Sir Simon de Wenslawe, a fourteenth-century priest, and Oswald Dykes, rector, who died in 1607.

For all its antiquity, the exterior of Wensley church has a remarkably clean-cut appearance, probably the result of restoration; the vertical lines of its tower, largely unbuttressed, are repeated in a well-kept churchyard where by some miracle headstones refrain from tilting. Fortunately, no designing hand has banished the greenfinch that sings the livelong day by the church gate, nor the rabbit that plays hide-and-seek among the gravestones; after all, he arrived, it is said, with the Normans, who first set up the building in 1245.

In a more elevated position, and mentioned in the Domesday Survey as 'Leborne' – the 'stream by the clearing' – the busy little town of Leyburn, capital of the lower dale, stands at the meeting-place of roads from Richmond, Reeth, Bedale, Masham, and Askrigg; it has a market charter dating from the reign of Charles II. In the largest of its three squares, the town hall, erected in 1856 by the then Lord Bolton, looks down on a town thriving as a centre of commerce and, in summer, of tourism. It has a wonderfully spacious market place, though the shambles, bull ring, stocks and cross are gone; its surrounding square of shops cater for all needs. In the early nineteenth century Leyburn was a meeting-place for the gentry. Social functions were held at The Bolton Arms Hotel; there were tea parties and a theatre, but no church until 1836. Rapid growth continued with the coming of the railway from Bedale in 1856. Today, especially on Fridays, with its market in full swing, the open spaces, once lively with sheep and cattle, are solid with traffic and stalls, the town welcomes dalesfolk, coach parties, holiday-makers, and servicemen from nearby Catterick.

From Leyburn, along the road to Masham, the dales landscape gives way to one of pastoral charm, with parkland, wheatfields, magnificent trees, and large, scattered farms. After Coverdale, only Colsterdale reminds the Yore of its ancestry in the high fells so many glorious miles westward. But the river has its moments, as it swings by the castled eminence of Middleham, with its Georgian houses and racing stables; then on by East Witton, and to Jervaulx, where, it is said, the monks first made 'Cover Bridge' (Wensleydale) cheese from ewes' milk, bred horses, and farmed the broad acres of the dale. The abbey was overtaken by the Dissolution, pillaged, and its abbot hanged at Tyburn in 1537. Over four centuries have passed since the seasons began to work their will upon it, and one sees it now as Yorkshire's most resplendent ruin, in a dale renowned for its scenic qualities.

XIII

THE EDGE OF BEYOND

Beautiful dale, home of the Swale,
How well do I love thee, how well,
Beautiful dale, home of the Swale,
Beautiful, beautiful dale.

IT is many years since I sat with Mary Alderson, in the kitchen of her cottage by the Swale. There at a plain-topped table, in a quiet punctuated by the ticking of a grandfather clock, Mary went lovingly through her collection of dales songs. To the gentle, tremulous voice of this white-haired daleswoman an accompaniment would have been an impertinence. Listening to her song, one felt a pang almost of remorse at one's intrusion; of inadequacy fully to appreciate her love of music, and of the dale of which she had been a part for almost eighty years. We went into the tiny front room to see her song books. A sash window splashed scarlet with geraniums looked out on other grey cottages, and above roof-tops to the scarred heights of Gunnerside Gill, where for generations the menfolk of Mary's family had worked in the lead mines. She had her recollections of those, too, and of the day when after an accident they brought her injured grandfather down the hillside, and the doctor performed a leg amputation on the kitchen table. "They just took him and they sawed it off, and I watched them; no anaesthetic – nothing! William Alderson, he was called; and he lived till he was over ninety. When his pals came round they were very tickled about the thought of his wooden leg; then they all got down to some singing!"

As music entered into the life of Mary Alderson, so the mining of lead has been a major theme in the story of a dale whose modern limits stretch from the city of Richmond to the borders of Mallerstang; somewhat more than those set forth in the traditional jingle – "the extent of Swaledale is twenty long mile". In medieval days the dale began at Reeth, on the edge of forest land unrecorded in the Domesday Survey.

The dome of the Askrigg Block, the upland mass between

Stainmore and Ribble, tilting eastward to give the dales their variety and individuality, has bequeathed to the Swale a dalehead of high fells of Millstone Grit – High Seat, Great Shunner, and Tan Hill. Around Keld, a number of waterfalls mark the terraces of the Yoredales, as at Kisdon, Catrake, and Wainwath. The landscape of this rhythmic combination of rocks is less spectacular than that of neighbouring Wensleydale, due to the dominance of shales and sandstones in the series. Limestone scarps occur at Wainwath, Kisdon Gorge and Oxnop, and the fluted vertical shafts of Buttertubs are well known to sightseers. Near Grinton, river meadows with a tendency to flood behind a bank of moraine provide evidence of a post-glacial lake.

At the dalehead Hugh Seat, High Seat, and Nine Standards Rigg, named after the distinctive group of stone cairns, are the gathering ground of many gills that unite at Little Moor to become the Swale – Uldale, the Sleddales, and Whitsundale Beck. High Pike Hill (2,105 feet) overlooks Lamps Moss which at 1,698 feet tops the pass to Mallerstang. Tailbrig, an area of pavement and peat hag, is of special interest ornithologically, with its breeding dunlin, golden plovers, wheatears, and pot-hole-nesting ring ouzels. In recent years trips of dotterel have been noted at 1,600 feet on the outcropped plateau, pausing briefly on their way north in April, May and June; less surprising are similar sightings at over 2,000 feet on High Seat. From the western edge of Tailbrig, seen across the Eden valley, the conical hills of Murton and Dufton often show clearly in sunshine, relieved against the dark wall of Crossfell (2,930 feet) and its neighbours, seldom without an attendant roller of cloud; among them is Mickle Fell (2,591 feet), Yorkshire's highest peak.

From the summit of the pass at Tailbrig comes the story of the killing in 1664 of John Smith, a pedlar, on his way from Swaledale to Kirkby Stephen. All traces of Hollow Mill Cross have vanished, but evidence remains of the murder there, and of the recovery of a body found nearby in a peat hag. Whether the motive was personal or political has never been established, though some have connected the incident with the Kaber Rigg Plot and the execution of the Mallerstang 'stockinger' John Atkinson, a Commonwealth supporter.

A few miles down dale, Birkdale and Angram Commons are

dominated by Great Shunner Fell in an apparently limitless landscape whose aspect is as wild as its names – Knoutberry Currack, Hush Gutter, Lodge Hags, and Ravenseat – though some caution is advisable in the assessment of their meaning, which may not always be as obvious as one thinks. The naturalist, having viewed the craggy fells to the north, may be deluded, for example, by 'Ravenseat', whose origin could be without any ornithological implication; a derivation from 'Rafen-saetr' may well make it nothing more exciting than the spring shieling of the Norseman 'Rafen'.

South of Ravenseat at 1,600 feet is Birkdale Tarn, which once supplied water to nearby mines. Here a colony of black-headed gulls nests annually, though as is usual at such sites, numbers may vary from year to year. It is a short scramble from the Kirkby Stephen road to the edge of this surprisingly clear pool, but from the west approach can be damp and difficult, across a wet flush, to boggy margins where the birds nest. Perhaps the best view of Birkdale is from Thwaite Common, on the northern edge of Great Shunner Summit, where the prospect includes half of Swaledale. This is not the most spectacular of hills – bent, rushes, and cotton grass, in a gentle but prolonged slope from Buttertubs Pass, the quickest approach to the summit. Beyond the eastern edge at 2,000 feet there is an interesting change in the topography of Great Shunner. A denuded waste of level ground, littered with bleached stones and pale green mosses that crunch beneath the feet, stretches away between enormous peat hags. As if to complete this moon landscape, a trio of stony columns stands erect before the final wall of the summit. There are others, of unusual size, on the slope below; indeed, both Great Shunner and its neighbour, Lovely Seat across the way, have been well endowed with beacons; but whether by forgotten dalesmen bound for forgotten mines at Fossdale, or by shepherds on their current perambulations, it is hard to say.

One man who knows more than most about these moors is Tom Tiplady, who farms at Scar House near Thwaite, and whose 'stints' or grazing grounds extend across the flanks of Great Shunner. Stints or 'gaits', predetermined in number, and varying according to vegetational quality, are allocated to farms for rough-grazing on moor-tops and commons between dales. On a bitter December morning after early snow I came

Sheep fair, Tan Hill

Sheep sale, Hawes

Smithy, Dent

Blessing of sheep at
Howgill near Sedbergh

Sheep shearing. *Left* Tom Tiplady at Buttertubs; *Below* In Coverdale

Stainforth Foss, Ribblesdale

Long Churn, with Alum Pot in the background

Holly Platt, an old coaching inn near Ingleton

Overgrown limestone pavement north of Ingleborough

The Howgills from Firbank Fell

Cautley, Vale of Rawthey

Gayle, Wensleydale

Spring in Bainbridge

Smelt-mill chimney and flue, Cobscar, Wensleydale

Calver Hill, Swaledale

upon Tom carrying hay to his Swaledales, newly returned to
the moor after being put to the tup. *Lish* (active) and wind-
blown, he told me with a wry smile of the trouble and expense
involved when winter begins early; of the extra visits to the
moor, sometimes twice a day, in extreme conditions, and with
an added feed bill of several hundred pounds. Occasionally
ewes, which instinctively seek the shelter of a wall or peat hag,
become snowed in, and, if on their feet, often survive for up to
a fortnight. Sheep packed together, especially those in a hole,
may drown or become crushed; in extremities, they will nibble
at each other. After a few days, the heat from their bodies melts
the snow around them, a round hole appearing at the surface.
Fully trained dogs are invaluable in 'setting' buried sheep, and
young dogs are taken along to watch and learn. Strong winds
and snow can affect the behaviour of the flock, which, following a bad weather forecast, may be brought down to enclosed
land at the edge of the moor.

Conditions in the valley are somewhat better. "Wi 'ave a
deep freeze now; wi never 'ave any trubble. Milk goes iv'ry day
to Northallerton, and 'e's only missed once in sixteen years."

Lambing begins about 10 April, after the ewes have been
taken down to bottom land for a bite of meadow grass. Due to
improved methods and routine dosing, up to 20 per cent of his
ewes will produce twin lambs. 'Wethers' (males) will be
fattened and eventually sold off, 'gimmers' (females) may be
kept as breeding stock. In May, Tom turns out his forty milk
cattle for the 'early bite' of meadow grass, and sheep and lambs
are then returned to higher ground.

Fell sheep are usually 'heafed'. By this system a flock is
retained on its own ground, even though the farm may change
hands. The sheep become familiar with their own particular
terrain, and the shepherd usually knows where to find them.
Tom's flock tend to take to the heather between December and
February, and to 'moss ground' in late February or March, and
he reckons that one stint will support four sheep, two young
cattle, or one horse, though the latter have now been replaced
with tractors. Another advantage of the 'heaf' system is that
over the years flocks can build up an immunity to the parasite
infections peculiar to the terrain.

Stints or gaits are unfenced, and inevitably a few sheep
wander to another man's ground. In December, after the flocks

have been gathered for tupping, strays are taken to a Shepherds' Meet at Muker or Tan Hill, and restored to their rightful owner; unclaimed ewes are sold for a charity.

I called to see Tom one day in July after shearing time, hoping for a chat. In the jargon of his business-man counterpart in the city, Mr Tiplady was 'not available'. Scar House basked in its idyllic setting of wild roses and meadow sweet, its waterfall hushed and invisible behind a curtain of greenery. Swallows conversed on the edge of an open window in the barn. Is there any song more charged with the essence of summer? Two bronzed walkers bound for the guest house at Thwaite paused to admire the view of Kisdon Hill, with the temperature in the eighties. On the hillside, the sound of a mowing machine, and an occasional glimpse of Tom astride his tractor, laying low the swathes of grass and flowers in an irony of fragrance and fuel oil. I remembered his pronouncement made among the snows of Great Shunner in December – "It's a full-time job is farming."

The good folk of Swaledale have had two preoccupations, and now that lead mining has gone, they are left with one – sheep. A very special sort of animal, with a crown on its far horn and named after the dale whose Breeder's Association is dedicated to its improvement. As sheep go, the extremely hardy 'Swa'dle', with its black face and white muzzle and undocked tail, might be considered good-looking. To some dalesmen, it is the handsomest creature on earth. Each spring its devotees gather on Tan Hill and hold a fair in its honour. At the risk of being facetious, one might say that this is the only occasion when shepherds flock to see a sheep. The inn on Tan Hill, reputedly the highest in England, stands at 1,732 feet above sea level. On the May afternoon I came to it, West Stonesdale was bathed in sunshine, but at the head of the gill a white mist hung over the moor top, driven by an east wind that conceded nothing to the season. On a knoll of moorland close by, the annual fair was in full swing. At the pub, to the sound of a brass-band, one is exhorted to "drink the Pennine Way". I ignored the notice, and passed along the row of stalls. If you find yourself in need of new shoes, this is the place to buy them. Or do you fancy double glazing? Or perhaps an ice-cream? (Perish the thought, in a wind like this.) Half the menfolk of Swaledale are here today, not to mention

Arkengarthdale and Teesdale. Trench macs, overcoats and cigars. Bustle and bleat; the flapping of posters that every moment threaten to tear themselves from the tradesmen's booths. One at least is weathering the storm. "Sheep can't tell one worm from another; you can!" To say one is flattered is an understatement. Forward to the sheep pens, and to blazes with the quoits tournament.

Inside the enclosure, and under clearing skies, the atmosphere is markedly different. There is a quiet earnestness about the faces that look down into the pens, a gravity in the quiet (and mutual) exchanges between man and sheep; the animals, coiffeured, consoled and condescending, are less concerned than their attendants. Horny hands clutch at wooden rails; sticks are brandished in emphasis; conversations wax and wane; snatches of esoteric intelligibility to the outsider. On the judging pad, a dalesman wrestles with an outsize ram as two judges stand back and confer, oblivious to the crowd of onlookers. It is all very intense, as befits the august animal whose likeness appears as the emblem of the Yorkshire Dales National Park. As one Swaledale veteran informed me, "Them's best sheep i't'world."

The inn at Tan Hill, lying on the Pennine Way between Keld and Stainmore, is known today to walkers and motorists, but was formerly the haunt of packmen, drovers, and colliers from nearby pits; ale, it is said, was consumed by the gallon, among a company not distinguished by its delicacy. The Tan Hill pits, which were worked as far back as the thirteenth century, supplied local domestic needs, and smelt-mills; coal went to Appleby, and Richmond, and to the Haverdale woollen mill in Swaledale. From the inn, a good road leads eastward over the millstone grit country of Sleightholme Moor to Reeth and Barnard Castle. It is impressive moorland, at its most colourful in November when the apparently endless grassland glows with the tawny hues of autumn. One can look towards Teesdale over a waste devoid of human presence; only the sharp-sighted will discern the line of moving specks at the horizon, as traffic moves over Stainmore. One night soon, after rain has fallen in the valley, will come the inevitable news that the first snow of winter has blocked the pass. Westward, the Tan Hill road winds across the plateau past conifers to Barras, Kaber, and Kirkby Stephen.

At 2,203 feet, Rogan's Seat is the centrepiece of the upland that encloses much of upper Swaledale, and along with Water Crag (2,176 feet), Friarfold Moor (1,931 feet) and Great Pinseat (1,914 feet), gives rise to a number of major becks, including Stonesdale, East Gill, Hind Hole, Gunnerside Gill, Hard Level Gill, and Arkle Beck. Peat moors of bent and rush, and some heather, grit outcrops, and bracken-covered hillsides that plunge down into gills scarred with spoil-heaps and the dereliction of mining, make up the landscape that surrounds this wild and deeply cut dale. In the upper dale the absence of lynchets, and village names like Keld, Thwaite and Gunnerside, indicate Norse settlement. Here the landscape has none of the venerable monastic ruins or noble parkland that have endowed Wensleydale and Wharfedale with much of their charm; Swaledale's ruins are of smelt-mill and quarry, and its trees cling to gill and steep hillside to give a wilder beauty. On intake slopes, where machines cannot operate, grass may still be cut and raked by hand, and the steepest banks and corners, untouched, become flowery sanctuaries, where melancholy thistle, scabious, ragwort and knapweed bloom and butterflies congregate. In one such corner not far from Muker, the butterfly orchis flourishes within a stone's-throw of the main road. Remarkable in the lower landscape and following the valley floor and hillsides are the numerous out-barns into which hay could be put directly, and where cattle could be over-wintered. A century ago haymaking was all done by hand, often by Irishmen, many of whom brought their own scythes. Work began at 4 or 5 a.m. after bread and cheese and a jug of milk; breakfast was about 8. A dewy morning, with some cloud, was preferred, and liquid refreshment in the form of a barrel of beer was usually supplied. After the hay was dry, cocked and windrowed, it was carried by sledge or sweep and pitchforked through the hole and into the barn. Milking was done in the fields and the milk carried home in a back-can, worn like a rucksack; older dalesfolk still remember as children being given a drink of warm milk from a back-can lid, out in the fields. In the lower dale, where more dairy farming is done, new features have appeared in the landscape as silage towers; prefabricated outbuildings, and hygienic milking parlours reflect new methods of milk production; the milk tanker, which collects in bulk, is now an added (and often unexpected!) hazard along narrow dales roads.

From Great Shunner Fell the Pennine Way descends Stockdale to Thwaite and Keld, which lie at the foot of Kisdon Hill (1,636 feet), and isolated spur of Angram Common. Here the Swale bends sharply through a wooded ravine, stepped with the waterfalls of Catrake, East Gill, and Kisdon Force. These are linked by pathways which offer some of the most delightful walking in the Dales. One track crosses East Gill and, skirting the gorge, gives a glimpse of the main Yoredale limestone at White Waller, with its hanging woodland of ash, birch, rowan, and sycamore. Along a lower path, and approaching Swinner Gill, progress can be difficult across overgrown spoil-heaps; nearby, equally overgrown, are the ruins of the Beldi Hill smelt-mill, where a water-wheel, now ruinous, once operated bellows for the hearths. On the hillside above, Crackpot Hall, a solidly built farmstead, was occupied until 1953. Those who wish to cross the river may do so by a small suspension bridge which leads to Hartlakes, to more deserted homesteads, and to Kisdon Force or Muker.

Most visitors come here in summer, when the little backwater of 'Appletree Keld' is chock-a-block with cars, ice-cream at the post office is the order of the day, and walkers rest in sunshine outside the youth hostel. But there are other sunny days, in November, perhaps, when the face of White Waller is suffused with yellow light, and the afternoon sun can no longer lift above Kisdon Hill. In the croft behind the chapel two Swaledale tups tug at the chain that unites them and await the arrival of the ewes. While a last shaft of sun reaches East Gill, Kisdon Force is a mere voice in the gloom; bracken and birches in West Wood, above the line of shadow that will soon engulf them, glow with fire. As the sun dips, a flock of redwings, which all day have moved indecisively about the hillside, pitch suddenly downwards as with one accord into the gloomy depths of Kisdon Gorge. In the last light and under gathering cloud rack, the hills move closer above the roof-tops of Thwaite. It is in these shortening days, towards the end of the year that one recalls with pleasure visits in high summer, when ring ouzels skulk among green bracken and orchids beautify the path to Crackpot Hall.

The stream that waters Stockdale is full of caprice. As Thwaite Beck it approaches the village, and frolics over its rocky bed and beneath the bridge. Joined from the south by Cliff Beck, which also celebrates its arrival in the dale as it pours through an attractive limestone grotto, it becomes Muker Beck, and is then absorbed into the more decorous Swale.

Those who enter Swaledale by Buttertubs Pass will be charmed by their first close glimpse of the valley, and will no doubt pause at Thwaite, with its handful of stone houses tightly gathered under Kisdon. To older country-lovers, the name on the sign of the shop and guest house will be sufficient to trigger off happy memories of the first nature books illustrated with photographs taken "direct from nature" – the work of two famous sons of the village, the naturalists Richard and Cherry Kearton.

Cherry, the younger, was to become a renowned wild-life cinematographer; Richard, famed for his many books on the countryside. Richard was born in 1862, of farming stock, at a time when lead mining was in its heyday, and horses and coal carts rattled backwards and forwards past the little school in Muker which he attended and which today displays a memorial plaque. At seven, the lad fell from a tree while birdnesting and was left a cripple; at eight, he was awarded a Wharton Bible. His love for nature never flagged. At twenty, after he had taken up farming, he met a founder of the publishing house of Cassell, and joined the firm in London. In 1892 the brothers began their photographic efforts, and in various disguises, including the now famous hollow ox, succeeded in producing wild-life "sun-pictures" for their books and lantern lectures. The Keartons were to become a legend in the annals of English natural history, and Swaledale a fitting background to the story. It is over forty years since I made the acquaintance of Richard Kearton's *With Nature and a Camera*, yet I must confess that in my own excursions on and around Great Shunner I can still never pass a stationary sheep without a smile and a backward glance!

To the south, this section of the dale is bounded by Lovely Seat ("Lunnerset") (2,213 feet), Blea Barf (1,772 feet) and Harkerside (1,676 feet). Major streams cut back into this upland – Oxnop Gill and Summer Lodge Beck. The former has a magnificent limestone scarp at its head, and a road that connects with Wensleydale, once a busy road between Muker and the railway at Askrigg; a cattle grid on the modern tarmac road marks the site of Jenkin Gate, an inn once popular with travellers, hauliers, and miners. Across the watershed, grouse moor atop limestone outcrops stretches eastward over Whitaside. A tarn set among peat and heather is noisy with black-headed gulls in spring and summer, which is a good time to explore the deep Bloody Vale that lies beneath Summer Lodge Moor. There is a Fairy Cave where a stream is born; a tumble of gritstone on the hillside; and wherever the hand of man has touched the earth in quarry or mine, a profusion of diminutive starlike spring sandwort covers spoil-heap and scree. At the foot of Oxnop Gill, Mill Bridge marks the site of one of Swaledale's many mills, and near Summer Lodge, once the property of Bridlington Priory, the hamlet of Crackpot also had its mill. Along the main valley, settlements succeed one another; Muker and Gunnerside are Norse in origin, and like many hamlets up-dale from Reeth, were augmented by miners' cottages at the end of the eighteenth century. Muker, set on a knoll on the hillside, is larger than the passing traveller might think. On a terrace behind The Farmer's Arms narrow ginnels lead among tiny gardens and an intimate collection of houses, many with an outside stair; such passages usually end at a field gate, opening on to meadowland, and with charming vignettes of the distant dale. A small shop and post office, hidden in the centre of the village, carries the signboard 'M. Guy' – a not unfamiliar surname in these parts. (The rest are Raws, Keartons, or Sunters!) In 1580 a chapel of ease of Grinton was built here, and close to it, a Literary Institute and Public Hall occupy central positions. In the latter, well appointed with a stage and equipment, social functions are held; here, too, the Silver Band practises. In summer one comes across their list of engagements, along with bands from Reeth and Richmond, posted on village notice-boards, recalling the days when Muker Band performed a marathon of concerts, travelling to Askrigg, Coverdale and Hawes, to play, and returning at night by way of Buttertubs. The annual show held in September is a popular event – a modern substitute for the traditional fairs once held in Thwaite and Reeth.

Gunnerside – "the pasture of Gunner" – stands by a crossing of the Swale where bridges have had a singularly unfortunate history, being liable to damage in times of spate; the ancient hump-backed pack-horse bridge, a mile upstream at Ivelet, has survived, as has the legend of its spectral headless dog, though the old road on the north side of the dale has been superseded by a modern one across the river. At Gunnerside, The King's Arms, the bridge, and an old smithy once run by the Calverts, attract many visitors. The more active may make the trip up the west side of Gunnerside Gill, where a most impressive concentration of derelict mines is to be seen. Here at Blake-thwaite, and over the moor at Old Gang, were two of the busiest lead-mining areas in the dale, and remains are to be found on every hand. Spoil-heaps litter the hills, and the ruins of workings, peat stores, flues and smelt-mills, of which Swale-dale had over twenty, are a frequent sight. Among these deep gills horizontal tunnels or 'levels' were driven into the slopes to work the veins; otherwise, on flatter ground, as in Wharfedale, entry was by vertical shafts. Deep grooves gouged into hillsides, as seen in Gunnerside Gill and on Fremington Edge, are the result of "hushing", a method of exposing veins by impounding and releasing an artificial torrent of water down a hill slope. The names of workings make interesting reading – Dam Rigg, Moulds Top, Friarfold, Hind Rake, and Sir Francis level, the last named after mine-owner Sir Francis Denys of Draycrott Hall, at Fremington.

The story of lead-mining in Swaledale goes back to monastic times, when Rievaulx Abbey held rights in the valley. Indeed, there is some earlier evidence in the form of pigs of lead of Roman origin, discovered at Hurst. The eighteenth century was the period of smaller prospectings, and six thousand tons of lead were produced annually. In the first half of the nineteenth century the industry, under larger companies like the A.D. and the Old Gang, reached its climax, involving over eight hundred miners, many of whom were housed in newly built cottages; in 1851, the population of Healaugh, for example, rose to 251. Today, it is around 40, and many of its cottages are owned by off-comers. Towards the end of the nineteenth century the industry failed due to imports of foreign lead, and a migration of workers to the collieries of Durham, or to the textile mills of Lancashire, took place. Today the old mining road and the scarred hillsides at Gunnerside Gill bear silent testimony to this colourful era of human activity in the Dales.

Of equal economic significance to the dalesfolk of past

centuries was the cottage knitting industry, of which Richmond was the centre. In 1724 Defoe wrote: "here you see all the people, great and small, a knitting". In 1820 Edward Stillman, minister at Keld, walked to London to raise money for rebuilding the chapel, knitting as he went. The pattern of the industry followed that of Dent and the north-western dales – knitting schools for children; stockingers; markets. By the beginning of the nineteenth century Reeth had become a busy centre for the stocking trade, and soon the dale had several mills for knitting processes. A small fulling mill was established about 1835 on Haverdale Beck by the Knowles family of Low Row, but ultimately the venture proved uneconomical, and the mill was demolished. Its chimney remained until about 1965, when it was pulled down and the stones used locally. A heap of masonry, overgrown by saplings of elm and sycamore, is all that now remains of the mill, but across the clearing, now a contractor's yard, a tall stone building with an outer stair accommodates a family in what was once the mill-workers' quarters. By the middle of the century a decline had set in, and in the years that followed, entire families of knitters joined miners in an exodus to Durham and Lancashire.

Seen from Low Row, the edge of Harkerside Moor, hard and uninviting, is notched along its skyline with the scars of 'hushing'. One passes unknowingly into Feetham, with its many small cottages strung out along the roadside, and an unexpectedly imposing inn, The Punch Bowl, marked 'A.D. 1638'; a goat browsing at the end of a rope on the green appears almost contemporary. Above the inn on the hillside a building known as 'Deadman's House' was used by bearers on the Corpse Road, who left their burden in its wicker basket while they repaired to The Punch Bowl to refresh themselves.

On the south side of the river, and rising over a hillside of juniper, the scenic road to Grinton is a route full of interest. The Swale, meandering through rich meadowland, is here spanned by a small suspension bridge known locally as 'Swing Bridge'. One notices particularly the myriad small enclosures reaching far up the hillsides; the long, narrow strips extending towards the river, giving each owner a share of 'bottom land', and access to water; and close by, the rich brown earth of arable land. To the west of Reeth, extensive lynchets on the north side of the valley, now absorbed into larger enclosures

recall medieval days, and the settlement from the east by the
Angles whose place-names extend as far as Feetham – Reeth,
Grinton, and Healaugh. Evidence of earlier times is to be seen
in an entrenchment, probably Romano-British in origin,
which runs down the slopes west of Dyke House on Harkerside, and which reappears across the valley at Fremington. Most
impressive of all is the overgrown defensive site or camp
known as Maiden Castle, which occupies a commanding
position on the hillside opposite Healaugh. Here one can
scramble up a slope of bracken and heather to a roughly
circular depression, almost two acres in extent, where a fine
rampart surmounts the deep entrenchment. Not the least
striking is the avenue of stones over a hundred yards long, laid
in parallel lines, which approaches the site from the east, where
there is a small tumulus.

In the twelfth century the dale became the property of
Walter of Gant, who established a hunting lodge at Healaugh,
and subsequently much of the land passed into the hands of
Bridlington Priory and Rievaulx Abbey. Traces of Norman
work still remain in the church at Grinton – the 'mother
church' of Swaledale, whose wide-flung parish once extended
to the Westmorland border, and to whose precincts came the
ancient Corpse Way. Much of the church is in the Perpendic-
ular style; the tower is of the sixteenth century. The building
has a 'Leper's Squint', and a copy of Birkett's New Testament.

The village of Grinton – the 'green settlement' – today gives
little idea of its importance in former days, when the weekly
market was held on Sundays for the benefit of those who had
travelled the length of the dale to worship at the 'parish town'.
Nowadays, visitors to Grinton may stay at the seventeenth-
century Bridge Hotel and enjoy its fishing, inspect the Bene-
dictine Marrick Priory, or walk the fells, perhaps over
Fremington Edge, to ponder over the desolation of mining at
Hurst.

Here at over 1,200 feet the desolation is complete. Miners'
cottages have disappeared, or lie in dereliction by a scarred
slope with two smelt-mill chimneys; one or two farms struggle
for existence on the edge of former mine workings. One cannot
help but view with amazement the endless spoil-heaps, and
marvel that human habitation is tolerable under such conditions. But in August there is some relief of colour when the

hay is gathered in, and the stony waste blossoms with trefoil, sandwort, and heartease; on dull days the visitors may be glad enough to escape from this uncompromising landscape, leaving Hurst to the grey skies and the wheatears.

Those who visit Grinton will certainly want to come to Reeth. It is not every day that you can take tea in a black-smith's shop, at the edge of a most delightful and spacious green, as you can here in the little capital of upper Swaledale, which in the heyday of mining and knitting, in the last century, enjoyed great prosperity as a market town. Like other dales villages, it had its annual fair held on 24 August – St Bartholomew's Day – when farm folk and miners from the surrounding countryside came into the village to celebrate. John Harland (1788-1875), a local dialect poet, described the attractions and gaiety of 'Reeth Bartle Fair':

> Thar was sizzers an' knives an' read purses,
> An' all sorts of awd cleathes o' t' nogs;
> An' twea or three awd spavin'd horses . . .

It is not without regret that one notes the passing of such occasions; nowadays, Reeth has its 'show' in September, and a sheep fair in October. Brass band and a women's institute are enduring features of its social life.

At the north-east corner of the village a road leads down to Arkle Beck, and in a pleasant little corner overlooked by hills, where once a corn mill operated, Mrs Postgate lives in the former miller's house, with its curiously projecting curved lintels – puzzling, until one realizes they are of old millstones. The fabric of the mill still stands, and one can still see the remains of a driving shaft, and the course of the mill-race, now covered with slabs; two iron grids once acted as sieves across the channel. Before electricity came to the valley, the mill had in its later days been fitted with a water-driven generator (erratic) and supplied power (grudging) to the village (over-optimistic). Hours of use were restricted, and street lighting non-existent. "Wi dreaded autumn," Mrs Postgate told me, "cus leaves got stuck in't grid, and all't lights went out!"

Once Reeth had a population of nearly 700; at present, with about half that number of residents, it is a popular centre, especially with tourists, and offers shops, cafes, accommodation, a choice of five hotels, and an excellent folk museum. On the

western edge of the village, there are some exquisite views of
river and moorland; Quaker Lane, a narrow raised path, leads
off towards the Swale.

Here about 1785 a Quaker school, now gone, was endowed
by Leonard Raw; nearby is the Friends' School, which ultimately replaced it. Nonconformism took a strong hold on the
valley, especially among the mining community, as is evi-
denced by the large number of chapels seen along the way in
almost every hamlet. After the Dissolution, much of the
upper dale became the property of the Whartons; in the late
seventeenth century, Philip, 'the good', Lord Wharton, gave
out Bibles, and as a Dissenter had had his effect upon the
dalesfolk, many of whom, as Seekers, had heard the message
of George Fox. He encouraged dissenting clergy, and endowed
a Protestant meeting-house at his shooting lodge at Smarber
Hall, above Long Row, where every August a commemor-
ative meeting is held. The Wharton Bible Charity, still active,
issues Bibles to children of the dale who have learnt certain
psalms.

In 1761 John Wesley was active in the dale – a little too
active, perhaps, for it is recorded that he sprained his thigh
running down a hill, and came to grief on his horse at
Whitaside while travelling to Low Row, where he found "an
earnest, loving, and simple people". The impact of Wesley
was considerable. Miners gathered in large numbers and sang
in the open air; meeting places were enlarged; and between
1789 and 1845 chapels were built at Reeth, Healaugh, Low
Row, Gunnerside, Muker and Keld. (Most of them still
flourish, and at more than one along the dale a well-known
bank has had reason to bless the influence of John Wesley.)

Near Grinton, Arkle Beck joins the Swale, and a spur of
Reeth Low Moor separates Swaledale from Arkengarthdale,
with its hamlets of Booze, Langthwaite, and Whaw. Here the
evidence of quarrying and lead-mining is at its most eloquent
in a brittle landscape characterized by its austerity. From
Feetham and Healaugh roads climb by Barney Beck beneath
the rounded eminence of Calva Hill (1,599 feet). At Mill
Bottom, from the remains of the smelt-mill, with its ruinous
flue and hearths, one can walk up Hard Level Gill to Old
Gang. The desolation is sublime. Yet it is not without some
relief that one seeks escape from this eerie, darkly petrified

landscape whose most disturbing feature is its silence. One emerges presently to wider skies and heather heights where bickering grouse call cheerily across the unrestrained horizons of Tan Hill.

XIV

THE ROAD TO THE NORTH

OF ALL THE PLEASURES that the Dales afford, those occasions
spent on the hills are often most memorable. From early days
one recalls the first scramble up Penyghent; a vision of wind-
blown ice-crystals on the summit cairn of Pendle Hill; and
the sombre moors of Brontëland, evocative

> In November days,
> When vapour rolling down the valleys made
> A lonely scene more lonesome.

Those who walk the hills will know that mist is by no
means the prerogative of winter, especially in a region like the
western dale-heads where the annual rainfall is of the order
of 100 inches, and where June and July can be the wettest
months of the year. According to one local wag: "Wi'v three
months winter, and nine bad weather."

On a day towards the end of May I found myself in mist
on Calders, in the Howgills, under just such conditions as
would seem to vindicate the foregoing truism. A blanket of
cloud enveloped the summit, separating two worlds; the one,
cold, grey, and silent; and the other, two thousand feet below,
busy with traffic bound for Morecambe and Blackpool. It is
curious that when the mountain tops are hidden, what one
sees from below is cloud, of form and substance; yet enveloped in it, one is aware only of a dark and claustrophobic
translucence. The moment of descent when one unexpectedly
emerges from it, and the feeling of height occasioned by the
sudden presentation of distance, are impressive. On that
summer day as I came out over Middle Tongue, the vale of
the Rawthey hung like a green curtain framed in lingering
wisps of vapour. Against this backcloth the combe below
assumed an unwonted hollowness accentuated by the parallel
string-courses of sheep trods, and as the mist cleared the
bosomy contours of the Howgills became apparent. On the
fitful wind a brief and unexpected fragment of music came

174

faintly from the valley – the sound of a brass band at Sedbergh's annual gala. In the green and blossoming land below, now dappled with sunlight, springtime jollifications were in full swing along streets decked with bunting; a few hundred yards above me, a layer of grey cloud still bestrode the heights, and golden plovers brooded in the chill twilight world of Calders and The Calf.

In the panorama revealed from the head of Hobdale Beck, the vale of the Rawthey and the entrances to Dent and Garsdale are seen as a green carpet laid below the brown austerity of upland masses; it is not only the absence of drystone walling on the Howgills that strikes one, but the field boundaries of hedges at their feet. These give character to the western dales, especially at valley entrances and on lower ground; on hillsides and moor top walling is as impressive as ever, reaching far up the slopes, and often following the regular lines of gills that make Rise Hill and Baugh Fell distinctive. Indeed, it is the steepness and regularity of these two fells that make Dent and Garsdale so similar. Physically and historically the two dales have much in common. Their drainage is in the same direction, ultimately westwards, where lie their affinities; both are, to a large extent, dependent on Sedbergh and Kendal. On closer acquaintance, one becomes aware of some differences. Garsdale, less winding, and with little bottom land, is a main highway through the Dales, from Kendal to Leyburn; in the words of an official guide-book, it makes "an ideal motor run". Despite this somewhat dubious qualification, the dale is pleasant enough, though without the intimacy of Dent. The one might be represented as a quiet room; the other as a corridor, from which there is no retreat into side valleys if one excepts Grizedale. This absence of diversions is noticeable from the old Coal Road above Garsdale Stations; the dale, hemmed in by Rise Hill and Baugh Fell, and with new afforestation on its sides, curves gently from the watershed, embellished with the falls and rapids of the river, which as Grizedale Beck rises on Holmes Moss, close to the source of the Rawthey. Pursuing a deliberate and meandering course through the high hollow of Grizedale, the beck takes a sudden turn in the main dale to become the River Clough. The entrance to the side-dale can be easily missed, and its road climbs and curves over heather knolls to reach the shallow valley beyond. One remembers here the few lonely houses – one, a converted chapel – and their names; Rowantree, Flea Flow, and Flust. High summer comes late but exquisitely to the yesterday acres of Grizedale. In July, short-eared owls, having completed their breeding season, wander down the slopes of Baugh Fell, quartering the heather as they go, or, setting a long, high course for Widdale, pass over the bright patchwork of the hollow. By the beck, which is sometimes set almost formally in a narrow channel, a riot of golden hawkbits and ox-eye daisies is surpassed by orchis, and by regal melancholy thistle. There can be few more delightful and sequestered retreats than this one between Baugh and Swarth Fells; its name Gris-dale, the 'valley of the pig', is the least charming thing about it.

As in Dent, Garsdale folk live in widely separated communities whose names hint at their Norse origins; some of the houses, like Birk Rigg, date from the seventeenth century; East Brackenthwaite stands on the site of a grange of Coverham Abbey, which along with Easby and Jervaulx held property in the dale. At Raygill in 1734 was born the mathematician and apothecary John Dawson, who in his youth taught himself from books bought with his knitting money. John Inman, expert in nautical calculation, lived at Low Hall, in the middle of the dale. Reformers also had their effect; a Friends' burial ground, near Dandra Garth, recalls the visit of George Fox, and a number of Methodist chapels resulted from the influence of Jonathon Kershaw on the impoverished dalesfolk, who in the last century supplemented their income by knitting, quarrying, and mining. The remains of 'marble' quarries can still be seen at 1,500 feet on Rise Hill, and of coal pits above Garsdale Station. These latter were abandoned when from 1865 the new railway brought in cheaper and better coal. At Danny Bridge, where Silurian meets limestone along the line of the Dent fault, the Clough passes through a limestone gorge, and the remains of kilns in the area recall another era of dales life to which new roads and the coming of railways put an end.

There are more than thirty summits in and about the Yorkshire Dales which exceed 2,000 feet Mickle Fell (2,591 feet), on the edge of Teesdale, takes pride of place, but is far less known than Whernside (2,419 feet) and Ingleborough

(2,373 feet). Well down the list, and little visited, is Baugh Fell (2,216 feet). Few people, it seems, consider it worthwhile. It is unspectacular, somewhat regular shape, and not particularly impressive as a viewpoint. To the ornithologist it has the recommendation that the dotterel has been recorded there, in recent years, as late as mid June, which might suggest the possibility of a breeding record; the passage during late April and May of 'trips' of birds along the various summits and high places is not unusual. There are records of birds from Pendle Hill, Ingleborough and Whernside. From the point of view of the naturalist, a visit to Baugh Fell could prove interesting, and the gentle ascent from Garsdale Foot is an easy approach, though the route is not nearly so delightful as its name would suggest. 'Ringing Keld' *is* one of those descriptive masterpieces in which the Pennines abound, and one cannot help but feel that half an hour with a glass and a map is time well spent. There you will find names that are lyrical, whimsy, or downright diabolical - though, perhaps, patently not always intentionally. Some are overtly descriptive; others tell us little of the places, but a good deal about the folk who named them - Throstle Nest and Appletreewick; Crackpot, Kettlesing, Booze and Jericho; Whaw, Catholes and Fiendsdale.

An hour's steady walking up Ringing Keld gutter will see one by the summit cairn of Baugh Fell, with its extensive views of the Howgills and Swarth and Wild Boar Fells, the latter seen 'end on', and therefore not to best advantage. East Baugh has a lesser high point at Tarn Rigg Hill, and the roughly triangular summit plateau thrusts a long arm northward to West Baugh. There are a number of small tarns and areas of broken ground which would appear attractive to wading birds generally, and to dotterel in particular, though the latter prefers a more elevated site for breeding. Whatever Baugh Fell may lack in height is, however, more than offset by the dotterel-hunter's greatest attribute - that of optimism!

Two miles from the dale head at Raygill we pick up once again the thread of the Settle–Carlisle railway. Emerging from Rise Hill Tunnel, the line passes high along the valley side to Garsdale Station, once known as Hawes Junction. Here in 1878, after much delay, a branch line to the North-Eastern Railway covered the remaining miles to Hawes, in neighbouring Wensleydale, to link with the Midland at Garsdale. A large complex was planned, but much of it abandoned. The station did, however, eventually boast a small engine shed, a turntable for re-routing the many pilot engines used in double heading, and a 43,000-gallon tank to feed the water troughs. A substantial, if incongruous, terrace of stone houses was built for railway employees, and the station became a focus of social activities for workers and dalesfolk alike. The turntable and sidings are gone; the engine shed, destroyed by fire; the branch line, lifted; and diesels have replaced the water-hungry locomotives that drank from "the highest troughs in the world". Today the station is a shadow of its former self; powerful expresses roar through unassisted, and in the darkness light from carriage windows briefly illuminates the platform sign 'Garsdale', in the midst of nowhere. To most travellers, on their way to more 'civilized' regions, this will convey little. In one sense, it is a good thing that trains no longer stop hereabouts, for it would be no joke to alight at the wrong station in these parts, especially in winter!

At the head of Garsdale, beyond the Dandry Mire viaduct, lies one of the major watersheds of the dales. An old inn, The Moorcock, newly opened after long closure and once known as The Guide Post, stands at the junction of three valleys. Here at the roadside an annual fair and a sheep and cattle show were held, attended by local folk from Garsdale, Wensleydale and Mallerstang. A little way to the north lie the sources of the Ure and Eden, which separate on their respective courses from the Aisgill watershed, famous among railway enthusiasts as a viewing point at the occasional re-incarnation of steam trains. On the embankment here a large gathering assembled on a poignant occasion in August 1968, when the Pacific locomotive No. 70013 'Oliver Cromwell' brought to an end an era which had begun with the arrival of the first passenger train in May 1876 along this, the highest main-line track in Britain. Indeed, the upper part of this dale, which presently becomes Mallerstang, is dominated by the railway, which with its many cuttings, tunnels, and embankments begins its long descent towards Carlisle. Passengers along this most scenic route complete the ten-mile section from Garsdale to Kirkby Stephen in as many minutes, which in some ways is regrettable for the wild beauty of Mallerstang is a thing to be savoured.

Dominant on its western side is the spectacular edge of Wild Boar Fell (2,324 feet), its edges of millstone grit thrust out above the valley. Seen from the tiny barnlike church at Lunds, or from the northern end of Mallerstang, its level top and scarp are distinctive enough – two straight strokes of a pencil would be sufficient to convey the likeness of this archetypal Pennine. Yet from the hamlet of Outhgill, one gets the illusion that the fell has unaccountably tilted backwards as if leaning on the wind. Its shattered crags, that run for more than a mile along the valley, are matched on the eastern side of the dale by the extended lines of Mallerstang Edge, and above them High Seat (2,328 feet) and Hugh Seat (2,257 feet) are high points of a plateau that inclines towards the head of the Swale. It is said that the latter eminence was named after Sir Hugh de Morville of Pendragon Castle, who held the manor in the reign of Henry II, and who was involved in the murder of Thomas à Becket. In the second half of the seventeenth century the dale passed into the hands of the Lady Anne Clifford, whose farflung estates extended from Skipton to Brougham. This indomitable, pious and ubiquitous lady, in defiance of Cromwell, repaired or rebuilt much of her property, including her castles at Appleby, Brougham, and Brough, and several churches. She set up almshouses at Appleby, and restored those at Bethmesley. Nor was she slow to commemorate her works, and the area has many mementoes in stone and marble to remind us of her presence and charitable deeds. Even now, more than one old dalesman will recall being admonished in his early days with the words: "Lady Anne won't like it!"

Some way down-dale, and close to the river, is Pendragon, which legend associated with Uther, father of the mythical King Arthur. The picturesque ruins of the castle, sprouting with young ash trees and set on a green mound, stand behind an overgrown moat and causeway. A more delightful situation is unimaginable. In summer, sheep group themselves around the stonework, still sufficiently intact to preserve the form of doorhead and arched windows, and the lines of Wild Boar Fell, framed among leaves, complete a tableau as idealistic as any landscape of Claude; in the eighteenth century it was drawn by Pennant. Whitaker described it as being "romantic

in name and situation". However tenuous may be the legend of
Pendragon, the castle is real enough. Its origin is probably as a
twelfth-century keep, repaired in 1300, and twice burnt by the
Scots, the last time in 1541. As a part of the Clifford estate, it
was rebuilt by the Lady Anne in 1660, who records in her
diary the setting up of an inscription to that effect over the
entrance. It reads like the credits of a television spectacular:
"This Pendragon Castle was repayred by the lady Anne
Clifford, countess dowager of Pembroke, Dorset, and
Mongomerie, baronesse Clifford, Westmorland and Vescie,
High Sheriffesse by inheritance of the County of Westmorland,
and lady of the honour of Skipton in Craven in the year 1660;
so as she came to lie in it herself for a little while in October
1661 . . ."

Two years later, Captain Robert Atkinson, a former
Governor of Appleby Castle and tenant of the Lady Anne,
whom she described as her "great enemy", and who lived
nearby at Dale Foot, was involved in an uprising to bring
about the retention of the Commonwealth. He was the leader
of the local insurrection, which became known as the 'Kaber
Rigg Plot' after the locality north of Kirkby Stephen where the
unsurgents met unsuccessfully. The plot foundered, and in 1664
Atkinson was executed at Appleby.

Mallerstang, whose name, it is said, derives from 'Mallard's
Stank' – the pool of the wild duck – is a through valley
running north and south, and as such has always been a
gateway to the Yorkshire Dales, especially for raiders from over
the border who swept down the Eden valley. The Scots were
troublesome between the eleventh and the fourteenth centuries,
when raids were particularly devastating. A number of castles
were built to afford some protection; at Appleby, Brough,
Hartley, and Pendragon. On the west bank of the Eden at
'Watter Yat' (Water Foot), the remains of Lammerside Castle,
possibly an early residence of the Wharton family, resemble the
shell of a derelict barn. Fortified houses, like Wharton Hall,
near Kirkby Stephen, provided a refuge during these forays.
This early fifteenth-century house, with towers flanking a
central hall, was enlarged in the mid sixteenth century by
Thomas, Lord Wharton, who added a new hall, kitchen,
courtyard and gatehouse block to make the whole a strong
defensive unit.

Among the notabilities entertained at Wharton Hall were, in 1568, Mary, Queen of Scots, on her way to Castle Bolton in Wensleydale, and in 1617, King James; as a result of the lavish reception of the latter, Lord Wharton was almost beggared.

In the second half of the seventeenth century the Scots began a further movement into the Dales, which was to last until the coming of the railways in the nineteenth century. This time, the incursions were peaceful ones, and were made by cattle drovers who brought thousands of Scottish beef cattle for fattening on the rich pastures of the Pennines. English graziers, like the Birthwhistles of Skipton and the Pratts of Wensleydale, travelled widely in Scotland to fairs or 'trysts', to buy stock from as far away as the Hebrides. The beasts, perhaps a hundred at a time, were driven unhurriedly along recognized hill tracks and river crossings. One such route crossed the shoulder of Crossfell and led by way of the Eden to Brough Hill fair, and thence through Mallerstang to Craven. The drives took place usually in September, and drovers and their lads worked in relays; sometimes they would be met south of the border by the buyer who conducted the herd to pasturage in the Dales. From these gatherings or fairs the cattle, having been fattened, were sent south, or disposed of at local markets, like Settle; other routes led to Wensleydale and Swaledale. Droving came to an end in the mid nineteenth century when animals were moved by rail to markets along the new routes of communication.

From Shaw Paddock at the dale head, to the Thrang near Outhgill, an ancient track, once a Roman road, follows a broad terrace along the eastern hillside, grassy and well defined along the section north of Devil's Bridge, where it crosses the deep limestone gorge of Hell Gill. Here in a narrow cavernous fissure of unexpected depth the beck rages down, and plunging over a sill of rock, spectacular in times of spate, is joined presently by Ais Gill to become the Eden. Down Mallerstang settlements follow the valley floor, with concentrations of houses at Outhgill, Castlethwaite, and Nateby, but south-eastwards from the head of the Ure a line of higher farmsteads – High Hall, High Way and Shaw's – are strung out along the track to Cotterdale.

Like so many other place-names in the area, that of Kirkby Stephen reflects the Norse influence, though remains and earthworks at 'Croglam Castle', a hill south of the town, and others at Waitby, Asby, Wharton and Nateby, indicate settlement of a much earlier date, possibly Bronze Age. Once a medieval market town, and subsequently a receiving centre for knitted goods, especially stockings, Kirkby Stephen's position south of Stainmoor on the trunk road to the Lancashire coast justifies its importance as a modern staging-post, much as it did in the early days of the turnpikes when The King's Arms was a coaching-house. Indeed, the busy little town, with its long main street, and cattle and outdoor markets, still has a touch of Georgian solidarity. Houses and shops stand back from the street, and in the season, throngs of holiday-makers from Newcastle to Blackpool crowd into cafes, eat fish and chips, or briefly explore the 'wynds' that lead off the main thoroughfare. Those visitors with more time to spare walk by the Eden, perhaps to the picturesque and flowery limestone gorges at Stenkrith, or make a tour of the 'Cathedral of the Dale'.

On the north side of the Market Square a gateway in the imposing classical façade of the cloisters gives access to the churchyard, where a flat tombstone on the right is known as the 'trupp stone'. Here on Easter Mondays until 1836 tenants placed their rent money in lieu of tithes of farm produce. Close by is the old Grammar School founded in 1566 by the first Lord Wharton and used until the opening of a new comprehensive school in 1955.

The parish church, possibly dedicated to St Mary, and standing on a Saxon site, is an impressive building, and has been compared in beauty with Carlisle Cathedral. Its nave dates from 1220, and the tower from about 1500. On a stone slab is a pre-Conquest figure of Loki, the oldest Christian personification of the Devil, here depicted in chains. On the south side of the altar is the Hartley chapel, behind a modern glass engraving by John Hulton, whose work is also seen in Coventry Cathedral; it depicts the stoning of St Stephen. The chapel commemorates Sir Andrew de Harcla (Hartley), first Earl of Carlisle, who was hung, drawn and quartered without trial in 1323. His remains were gathered from Carlisle, London, Newcastle and Bristol by his sister, and a brass plaque marks the spot where he worshipped, and where, it is thought, his remains are interred. The de Harcla estates passed to the Musgrave family, and an altar tomb marks the resting place of

Sir Richard, who died in 1464, and who reputedly killed the last wild boar on Wild Boar Fell.

The Wharton chapel north of the main altar contains the effigy of Thomas, the first Lord Wharton; his head rests upon a tilting helmet, and by his side lie his two wives. If their likenesses are anything to go by, the two ladies were not blessed with good looks. A Latin inscription on the slab records their passing: " . . . the Whartons gave me my heritage, my conquering arm victories over the Scots". Somewhat less eulogistic is the humorous transcription:

> Oh, how can I speak without dread!
> Who could my sad fortune abide?
> With one devil under my head,
> And another laid close on each side!

Among other scions of the Wharton family resting here in the chapel is Philip, fourth Lord Wharton, a Presbyterian who in 1690 began the distribution of Bibles; one can be seen in the church of St Leonard at Chapel le Dale, near Ingleton, and many others found their way into the cottages of the dalesfolk.

There are few areas of the Pennines more steeped in history than this, but for most visitors it is pre-eminently an area of outstanding scenic appeal.

There is a grandeur about the birthplace of the Eden that few dales possess, a beauty as primitive as the names that men have coined for it - Mallerstang, Outhgill, Pendragon, and Swarthfell. It is completely without the seclusion of, say, Dentdale; Wensleydale's spacious reaches seldom give the impression of being dominated by its high ground. But Mallerstang is of sterner stuff, and its high places, so often lost in cloud, rise in a rocky wall on either hand. It is rough, untamed country, away from normal tourist routes, and under its wide skies, dark crags, and fells that stretch away northward to Stainmoor, the impact of man is minimal; from the heights, his houses, mines, collieries, and even his railway, are obliterated.

Occasionally in winter, when the bare bones of the landscape are exposed, there occurs a perfect day on the hills; crisp snow above, a cloudless sky bluer at the zenith than a redstart's egg, and the sun perceptibly warm in its extending arc. Seen from the triangular plateau of Wild Boar Fell, the headwaters of the Rawthey are lost in shadow except where pinpoints of brilliance on Baugh Fell catch the eye – a pendant of tarns strung on a silver thread of beck.

Along the summit edge, not dissimilar to that of Helvellyn in its element of sudden exposure, a snow cornice is beginning to break away above the chasm; a visible fracture runs irregularly along the edge of crags, a discoloured margin of older snow that will slip away presently, adding its debris to the litter of scree two hundred feet below. The heights of Wild Boar Fell have none of the sheer slab faces of, say, Penyghent; they run a mile or more along the western side of Mallerstang forming a wall of shattered rock with almost as much debris as in the hollow combe below. Here you may sometimes come upon a fox picking his way along the stony slopes; the neat imprint of his pad in the snow or the sound of a falling stone dislodged from the crag may be the first indication of his presence. Today there is little sign of life except for a solitary raven pursuing a high and purposeful course. The ice-bound ledges are deserted, even by the hardy Swaledales, which, with the instinct of 'heughed' sheep, seek the more sheltered grass slopes by Swarthfell, still in sunshine.

Towards the end of the afternoon a blue shadow moves obliquely down and across the crags, lengthening and accelerating according to the steepness of the hillside. Already road and railway have been swallowed up, and Little Ing and Elmgill are about to capitulate. At the summit a lengthening line of ultramarine shadows links a group of cairns with the edge of the scarp, disappearing into an ultramarine abyss; orange and vandyke tussock draw a web of transparent azure in exquisite detail across the white satin of frozen mosspool textured with a dusting of powdered snow. The eye devours it all, but with difficulty. In the surfeit of light and colour the nearer hills are dark, especially the loom of Cautley Crag, in perpetual mourning.

An even layer of mist hides the Eden, but above its level surface rise in miniature the whitened undulations of Great and Little Dun and Cross Fells. Southward in silhouette and similarly diminished, Ingleborough and Whernside have drawn closer together in mutual reassurance at the unexpected sight of their peers to the north. But the most magical effect in a day of magic has yet escaped notice, lost in the ethereal high-key of snow and sky. Below the waning sun to the south-west an orange radiance hangs as if suspended, a soft and luminous patch of light that hovers above the indeterminate limits of the land. The reflection of a westering sun caught in the waters of Morecambe Bay appears to emanate from the sky itself; it seems inconceivable that the horizon should be so elevated.

Now a rising moon adds a further element to a canvas that in its mystic undertones might have come from the brush of Samuel Palmer, and it is with reluctance that one has to leave the summit. Half a mile below a numbing cold strikes the limbs and a pedestal of ice on boot soles makes progress difficult. Set against the overhang of a peat-hag, icicles that two hours before were dislodged by the weight of a footfall are already forming – a row of shark's teeth devouring night in the snow-lined gully.

In its final descent to the valley floor Ais Gill carves out a considerable gorge in the hillside, now deep in snow and shadow. From the depths of the shadowy gully the gaze is directed as along a gunsight, and there, almost three miles away across the valley, a rounded eminence is caught by the setting sun, brilliant above its base of darkened hills. It is difficult to believe that the green July dome of Hugh Seat can assume such a delicacy of pink and lilac; that prosaic earth can take on the ethereal qualities of the sky itself; but such is the magic of the changing seasons upon our northern hills. Now on the brink of evening a star is trapped in the hollow of Swarthfell. Past and present draw close; a stone or two fewer beneath the frost shattered crags; the same shadow flooding across the flanks of the fell; and perhaps the Lady Anne rounding Cotter End and urging her stewards onward to make Pendragon before night-fall, as Mallerstang Edge turns lilac.

Time has a way of standing still on the hills; one feels it sometimes in September when horizons draw in and an uneasy silence pervades the Pennine grasslands. Here now on a winter evening, beneath the star and the violet sky, in the sanctuary of the hollow gill above the Eden, one is aware of this timeless-ness; it is all a part of the enduring magic of hill country.

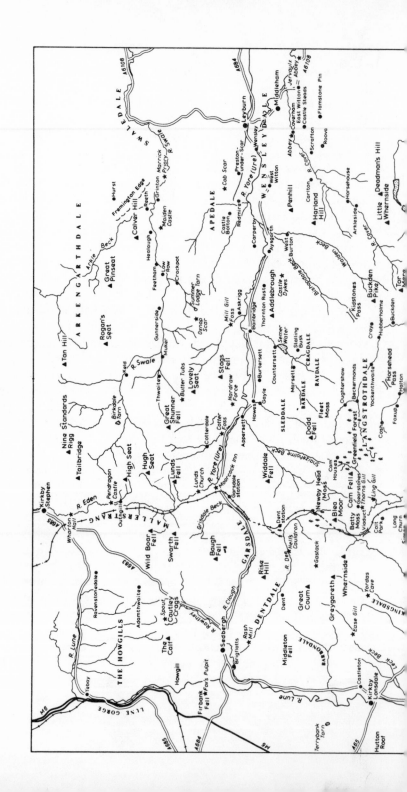

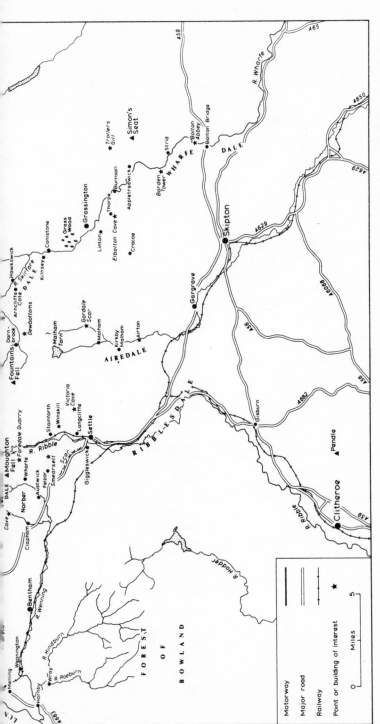

Based with permission on the Ordnance Survey

INDEX